CROSS-CULTURAL ENCOUNTERS

Bridging Worlds of Difference

LAWRENCE E. HEDGES

Listening Perspectives Press
ORANGE, California
2012 / 2023

Table of Contents

Bridges

What is it about a bridge that draws me? Perhaps it is the way it arches up, launches out, leaps for new ground. Perhaps it is the way even the most modest—an Andean bridge woven from osier, a slim ladder of slats—can swing out over an abyss, defy nature's will to divide. Even a vine—thrown from one cliff to another—is a miracle. It connects points that might never have touched. Perhaps it is simply that a bridge depends on two sides to support it, that it is a promise, a commitment to two. I love to walk a bridge and feel that split second when I am neither here nor there, when I am between going and coming, when I am God's being in transit, suspended between ground and ground.

—Maria Arana, *American Chica*

Table of Bridges

Perspective 8:
Samuel Beckett Bridge: Designed by Santiago Calatrava. Completed in 2009. Dublin, Ireland. Pen and Ink Illustration by Nora Kirkeby.

Perspective 9:
Khaju Bridge: Built by Persian Safavid king, Shah Abbas II around 1650 C.E. Isfahan, Iran. Pen and Ink Illustration by Nora Kirkeby.

Perspective 10:
Stone Arch Bridge built by James J. Hill for his Great Northern Railway Completed 1883. Minneapolis, Minnesota, USA. Pen and Ink Illustration by Nora Kirkeby.

Part II:
Sydney Harbour Bridge: Designed and built by the British company Dorman Long and Co Ltd. Completed 1932. Sydney Australia. Pen and Ink Illustration by Nora Kirkeby.

Part III:
Tunkhannock Viaduct (Nicholson Bridge): designed by Abraham Burton Cohen. Completed 1915. Nicholson, Pennsylvania, USA. Pen and Ink Illustration by Nora Kirkeby.

Part IV:
Alamillo Bridge: Designed by Santiago Calatrava. Completed in 1992. Seville, Spain. Pen and Ink Illustration by Nora Kirkeby.

Forward

This book is addressed to everyone who regularly encounters people from other cultural, ethnic, socioeconomic, linguistic, and ability groups. Its special focus, however, is aimed at counselors, therapists, and educators since their daily work so often involves highly personal cross-cultural interactive encounters.

Part I of the book defines a series of perspectives for considering cross-cultural interactions in professional and personal settings.

Part II of the book provides a series of actual cross-cultural encounters from the psychotherapy literature that give a close-up, slow motion picture, as it were, of various issues we are likely to encounter when we interact with people from diverse cultural backgrounds.

Part III of the book provides some in-depth psychological understandings of cross-cultural issues.

The running theme throughout the book is the importance of cultivating an attitude of tentative and curious humility and openness in the face of other cultural orientations. I owe a great debt to the many students, clients, and friends with diverse backgrounds who over the years have taught me how embedded I am in my own cultural biases. And who have helped me find ways of momentarily transcending those biases in order to bridge to an inspiring and illuminating intimate personal connection.

Introduction:
Caught in an Afternoon Thundershower

Achibe held aside the dense tropical leaves for me to pass. We had been walking for some time down a narrow path from the village market as the after-noon sky darkened over with clouds and thunder began rumbling overhead. As we entered the dark forest, the path widened slightly and Achibe took my hand—partly to lead me, partly because Ibo men often hold hands, and partly because apprehension was building in both of us as we neared the Awo Amama village shrine. Earlier Achibe had explained to me that this shrine was the abode of the tribal gods and the dwelling place of his ancestors. Achibe turned to silence me with a finger to his lips and we listened as wind began to rustle in the trees above and birds began wildly shrieking.

Having seen too many jungle movies, I wasn't sure what dangers lurked ahead but I could certainly sense Achibe's hesitation and fear. I had to remind myself that we were, after all, surrounded by a densely populated area, long since free of dangerous wild animals. And that Achibe had grown up here so that if there were any real dangers he would be alert to them.

Soon our way opened onto a small clearing with a firepit filled with ceramic shards in the center and a circle of well-worn logs on the periphery. We slowly walked the clearing in mesmerized silence peering into the surrounding thickets and searching the treetops for cackling birds and signs of spirits. After a while Achibe suddenly turned to me and, breaking our trance with a broad grin said, "Oh well, dead people can't hurt us anyway!" I was stunned by this brief glimpse into what he had been experiencing as I was taking in the mysterious strangeness of the place and the moment.

Raindrops signaled the afternoon shower as we opened our umbrellas and sat in reverent silence holding hands on a sheltered log to wait out the shower. Feeling the warm flesh of Achibe's hand in mine, the rush of the balmy tropical air, and the coolness of the falling rain, I sensed we were for a moment at that dizzying center point of a bridge—a bridge that can span the distance between two people, two cultures, two religions, two times, and two abodes—if we let it.

Since August of 1960 I have vividly remembered this intimate afternoon exchange with my Ibo friend, Achibe, as a symbol of how far our individual experiences can be from one another and how, for occasional moments, two people can bridge that distance and experience the warmth of human togetherness.[1]

This book is about some of the ways worlds of difference can be bridged.

---

[1] For fifty years Operation-Crossroads Africa, started by Dr. James Robinson of Church of the Master, Harlem, New York has been sending North American young people to spend the summer working in villages throughout Africa seeking to build bridges of friendship. In June 1960 I started out to visit the Belgian Congo but was waylaid in London because of the blood-bath there and instead spent the summer as the guest of Dr. Ben Nzeribe working at the secondary school he had established in his native Ibo village of Awo Amama, located in what was at that time the British Colony of Nigeria, Eastern Region.

My Multicultural Dream

After several years of intensive research and teaching multicultural issues, on the morning designated to begin actually writing this book I had the following dream:

> I was watching a couple traveling through heavy traffic in a large white van. At some point she agitatedly pushes herself back through the opening between the bucket seats into the rear of the van and onto a mattress with white sheets. She is wearing a seductive negligee with her hair loose— obviously feeling super-horny, begging the man to join her.
>
> Leaving the van moving forward in traffic, he too, agitatedly slips back onto the back mattress carrying some sort of riding crop or whip with many leather thongs.
>
> The two begin alternately embracing and kissing with wild passionate abandon and then playing master-slave games with him whipping her and her excitedly screaming for mercy.
>
> I am watching the scene through a cutaway from the upper front of the van. In my peripheral vision I see the now driverless white van continuing to career through heavy traffic toward a huge intersection with many roads and multi-colored vehicles converging from all directions.
>
> In the midst of his lusty whipping and her erotic screaming she manages somehow to raise herself to near standing position with her upper torso leaning out the rear window of the van screaming to the world for help—she wants free of this bondage game.
>
> A massive collision inevitably occurs at the crossroads with numerous vehicles of all colors and descriptions slamming into each other, wrecking

and overturning—with massive carnage, weeping, and wailing everywhere.

The dream ends as a nondescript man of some brown color—also observing from a cutaway portion of the van—points a finger at the white couple madly embracing in this frantic moment of high excitement, and loudly accuses, "You caused this accident!"

Sensing immediately upon awakening that the dream contains the key to my book project I begin free associating. There is the obvious white couple so passionately preoccupied with their dominance-submission games that they are totally oblivious as their large, aggressive white van ruthlessly ploughs through a world of multicolored vehicles toward a massive disaster at the crossroads.

But who was I in the dream—what God's-eye position was I occupying as I watched? And what about the accusing man of color? Who was he? What position does he represent? And what does his accusatory speech, "You caused this accident!" mean?

There is the obvious theme of oblivious racial victimization—but from my privileged place in the dream I could also see that those same oblivious dominance-submission games were being acted out in the back seats of the other driverless colored vehicles as well. Everyone was preoccupied with dominance/submission games. No one was taking responsibility for where they were going.

There is the obvious colored accusation and the potential for white guilt. But the colored man is not deeply invested in his accusation and the couple is too preoccupied to be feeling much guilt. So where is the action? In the dream I am not particularly impressed by the colored accusation or the white guilt either. It's as if everybody is in this together—passionately involved in dominance-submission games in the back seat—taking no responsibility for where they are going and for their inevitable appointment with disaster, carnage, wailing, and tears.

In pondering the meaning of the dream I realized that, like with so many features of our dreams, the accusation and the supposed guilt simply serve as background to the scenario, like the white van and the colored cars, like the bondage and discipline games and the white woman finally seeking liberation—they are all simply features that are part of the dream setting.

I suddenly fixed on "accident"—the last word of the dream that had awakened me. "Accident" suddenly seemed to contain the dream's emotional power and meaning.

What "accident," I wanted to know? Everything in the dream had seemed so obvious and clear—everybody's deliberate irresponsibility, the universal and willing mutual participation in bondage and discipline games, the casual obliviousness to the increasingly dangerous situation, the inevitability of the disaster, the stated accusation, the supposed "cause," and the presumed guilt.

From the God's-eye vantage point I occupy in the dream I ask, "What accident?" Why "accident"—the whole scenario seems so deliberate, so foreordained?

Could "the accident" be the long-ago migration to the north by certain tribes from central Africa?

Was the accident the European Ice Age with daily temperatures 20 to 40 degrees below zero that all but wiped out the northern brothers?

Was the accident the centuries of bitter cold that forced the invention of ingenious survival strategies in northern climes—inventions never dreamed of by brothers in the south or in others inhabiting less environmentally hostile migratory locations.

Was the accident the outcome of thousands of years of male competition and dominance in Europe—of countless ethnic wars over women and scarce survival supplies that forced additional cultural ingenuity onto peoples inhabiting in the inhospitable north?

Was the accident the increased needs for and uses of fire in the north, the search for sources of fuel, the necessity of winter hunting, animal husbandry, seasonal gardening, and the preservation of food for winter survival?

And what about the necessity for tight-knit social organizations of the endangered northern communities—the need for villages leading to property rights, male dominance hierarchies, and heredity rights?

Is the accident all the new rules and rituals required to sustain the precariously evolving northern lifestyle?

And what about the need for rulers and complex administration with written records to assure safety and success in the emerging northern way of life?

Was the accident our last three centuries of European socialization, education, urbanization, industrialization and militarization of nation-state organizations?

Was the accident the crowding of the European continent, the need for expansion, the discovery and colonization of the new world, the growing market demand for international trade?

Was the accident the European expanding trade that required more labor in America—trade that led to indentured servitude of impoverished Europeans in the American colonies, to the importation of African bond-labor, to trade involving indentured Asian agricultural and railroad coolies escaping famine in China?

Was the accident the invention of the "white race" during the eighteenth century in the Chesapeake Bay Colony where indentured Europeans were needed and recruited to manage bonded Africans on outlying satellite plantations?

In short, in considering my dream I realized that the entire rise of Western civilization along with the prejudice, bigotry, domination and exploitation it has spawned has been a gigantic series of historical "accidents"—yes, in a certain sense, "caused" by the pale skinned northern brothers.

But despite the well-known atrocities of pale members of the human race, the dream seems to ask, "Is there truly white guilt any more than any other color of guilt? After all, didn't male dominance and female submission follow us all out of Africa where female excision is still practiced today?" "Hasn't the survival instinct, male competition, and aggressive tribal warfare as well as abduction of women and children and the enslavement of conquered peoples characterized homo sapiens everywhere from our beginnings?" "Didn't our African and migrant ancestors systematically wipe out all other competing hominoids on the planet and extend our dominance-submission dominion to all life forms and material resources everywhere?"

"Don't we now see all life on Earth threatened by oblivious human lust and aggression as we collectively hurtle toward seemingly inevitable planetary disaster at the approaching crossroads of cultural and ethnic meetings?

Yes, in some important sense it's all an "accident." And yes, the looming disaster has been set up, "caused", if you will, by the cultural developments necessitated for human survival in northern climates—by the pale skinned brothers, as it were. Considered from this angle, the fated and fatal "accident" is nothing less than the inevitable march of human progress itself.

One might say, then, that the "accident" is the human capacity for symbolization, for speech, for abstract thought, for tool usage, for resource exploitation, for personal identity development, for transgenerational transmission of cultural inventions, and for massive technological advancement—technological advancement that has benefited us all—while simultaneously making possible atomic warfare and various forms of global destruction.

In short, the very things we pride ourselves most for as human beings can all be seen as parts of a gigantic accident with a global catastrophe just waiting to happen! All of this without our fully taking responsibility for where we are going. What hope do we have of salvaging the human race, of preventing the total destruction of life on planet Earth? We are all concerned.

In seeking to answer these questions I wrote this book:

- To consider what possibilities we have for ending male dominance and destruction on the planet, for ending racial, religious, political, and economic dominance, exploitation, and warfare;

- To consider how we can end all forms of colonization of human minds and bodies;

- To consider how we can work toward equal opportunity for all people, toward democratization of peoples everywhere, toward global peace among all people, toward protection of all life on Earth, and toward mastery of a sustainable environment;

- To consider how as professional counselors, therapists, and educators we can meaningfully engage in Cross-Cultural Encounters that can work toward Bridging Worlds of Difference.

I am a psychologist-psychoanalyst who has explored these questions for a lifetime in various contexts in Africa, South and Central America and in various places in Europe, North America and Australia. Further, I have taught multicultural sensitivity in numerous university and professional school settings and engaged in forty years of continuing education with mental health professionals that have always included cross-cultural issues.

This book is addressed to everyone who seeks ways of building bridges between personal worlds of difference. But it especially targets practicing counselors, educators, and psychotherapists. The case examples chosen are from the psychotherapy literature because in long-term psychotherapy the issues involved are often seen with slow motion clarity. I hope you enjoy considering these issues with me and that you find the examples of cross-cultural bridging provided here illuminating.

Larry Hedges,
Modjeska Canyon, California

Part I:
Perspectives for Considering
Cross-Cultural Encounters

General Considerations

Perhaps you've been questioning what reading this book will bring?

- "Will I learn about Chinese, Eskimos, Africans, Racism, colonialism, sign language, interpreters, or transgenerational ghosts?"

- "Will I feel forced to see how bigoted I really am?"

- "Will I learn how to survive as a professional in today's expanding multicultural climate?"

- "Will I learn what it means to consider counseling, education or psychotherapy in a cross-cultural context?"

- "Are our Western views of normality, pathology, diagnosis, ethics, and therapy even applicable to people from other ethnic groups and cultures?"

- "If it is true that we can expect more and more people from different language and culture groups to be showing up in our consulting rooms and classrooms in the future, how do we rise to the challenge?"

- "What, if anything, do we as counselors, educators and therapists have to offer to immigrants, to the poor, to the disenfranchised, to the culturally and ethnically dislocated, to those suffering from cultural shock, to those fleeing persecution and genocide, to those straddling conflicting cultural and ethnic demands, to the 'huddled masses yearning to be free?"

We start our adventure to consider cross-cultural encounters like we do all learning experiences—on the premise that knowledge is power. That knowing more in the multicultural arena will allow us a greater sense of certainty and security in our work with diverse populations.

But the mere mention of power in a multicultural context puts us immediately on alert. What kinds of power exactly are we seeking by reading this book, by attempting to learn more about other people who are different from us, and how to bridge those differences? What exactly might our power goals be?

What kinds of certainty and security in cross-cultural encounters do we feel we need? And why? Certainly, knowledge, and power have been used to subjugate, exploit, and dominate for thousands of years. What are our personal purposes in considering multicultural issues and what questions do we personally bring to our study?

Four Approaches to Developing Cross-Cultural Sensitivity

1. The "modern" approach, to cross-cultural competence is to learn the history and shared characteristics of various cultural groups. But this approach to cross-cultural "knowledge" implies that definitions and categorizations of culture are somehow known, static, monolithic and/or knowable.

2. A more contemporary "postmodern" approach considers culture and ethnicity as "always contextual, emergent, improvisional, transformational and political"—a matter of ongoing discourse and continuous change (Laird 1998). This approach values "unknowing" or a "lack of competence" as the avenue towards developing greater cross-cultural understanding.

3. An "intersubjective" or "relational" approach to cross-cultural, co-created competence implies that the thoughts and feelings of any two people form an interactive field that operates on many levels as two work together toward establishing mutual trust and co-constructing meanings.

4. A "sociopolitical" approach to cross-cultural competence considers the interplay between

    • the actual social forces of oppression, discrimination, prejudice, and lack of economic and political opportunity, and

    • the internalized characteristics and identities of those individuals, families, and groups continuously subjected to various forms of oppression (Green 1998).

Some Preliminary Definitions

"Cultural" and "ethnic" are interrelated concepts. For the purposes of this book I will use the terms: (a) "cultural" to accent a cohesion or correlation of ideas, attitudes, and practices and (b) "ethnic" to accent geographic origins—either regional or national, which may or may not include physical or sociocultural features.

The concepts of "race" and "racism" will be considered later in their historical and scientific contexts. The bottom line is that today we know there is one race—the human race—that migrated out of central Africa several million years ago and settled in all parts of the world. We live in a world of expanding identities and voices. Our thought and speech needs to reflect our changing realities. Changing our racial and ethnic vocabularies reflects our understanding of current realities. We are now gradually eliminating all racial terms—e.g., "white," "black," "people of color," etc., unless we are explicitly indicating that a particular person identifies her- or himself as Irish, Black, Cambodian, Eskimo, Iroquois, or White. Instead, we are coming to designate people by nationality or by their regional, national, or ethnic origin—such as African-American (Afro), Euro-American (Euro), Korean-American (Korean ancestry), Native-American or First Nation (American Indian)—not simply to be "politically correct" but to mark our changing cultural and global realities. Our thoughtful approach to multicultural awareness is a movement toward consciousness-raising about what is going on in the real world around us and where the human race is going. The point these days is not to eliminate difference, but in our speech and thought to highlight differences as facts without prejudice.

According to the 2000 U.S. Census:
- 35.3 million people are Hispanic
- 33.9 million are African-American
- 10.5 million are Asian or Pacific Islander
- 2.1 million are Native American

That is, 29% of the American population is Hispanic, African-American, Asian, Pacific Islander, and Native American and the percentage steadily rises.

Our goal in cross-culture encounters is bridging the gap that exists between people. Bridging involves shooting for the dizzying exhilaration that comes from attaining the mid-position on the bridge, from being able to see each side of the gap with some clarity, from knowing that there are two sides and that with help we can manage somehow to negotiate our way from one side to the other.

Bridging worlds of difference involves achieving a certain sense of mastery that comes from experiencing oneself between separate and different worlds and yet being cognizant of both sides. Building multiple bridges, creating diverse opportunities, inhabiting pluralistic universes—that is our challenge in cross-cultural consciousness-raising today.

The long-standing American idea of pouring everyone into the same melting pot mold has undergone a radical shift in recent decades. The current metaphor of cultural and ethnic mosaic honors various group cohesions and solidarities while at the same time recognizing differences. "We are all multicultural human beings; our very selfhood and identity are embedded in the language we speak, our gender, our ethnic/racial background, and our individual life path and experience" (Ivey et al. 2001, p. 1).

Three Approaches to Culture:
Evolutionism, Universalism, and Relativism

Multiculturalism raises the question of how valid or useful are the constructs of Western psychology when considering cross-cultural encounters. A simple example to illustrate this problem is the concept of "self" considered in a multicultural context.

- "Evolutionism as applied to [the self in psychology] posits definitive norms for what healthy human nature should be and how it develops. Invariably, these norms derive from a contemporary normative model of the individualized self as formulated in current [Western psychological] theory, and are assumed to be universal and superior....

- "The second approach to assessing the universality and variability of the self in different cultural settings is essentially to search for universals only. Difference or variability is seen as only superficially colored by culture....

- "The third theoretical approach for evaluating the universality and variability of [a concept such as] self in diverse settings is relativism. In relativism, as applied to psychological phenomena, highly differing views of human nature in different cultures are present, but these are viewed within an entirely different framework from Western individualism (Roland 1996).

Multiculturalism is emerging as a "fourth force" in psychology to supplement and ideally strengthen the three historical orientations of humanistic, behavioristic, and psychodynamic psychology.

Multiculturalism as a fourth force combines the alternatives of universalism and relativism by explaining behaviors by people from different cultures as simultaneously similar and different....People are similar in being driven by positive expectations for truth, respect, success, harmony, and positive outcomes that provide the universal values shared across cultures....[and] People are different to the extent that each culture teaches different behaviors to express those universal expectations....An inclusive, multicultural, fourth force perspective [in psychology] recognizes that similarities and differences coexist.... [The Multicultural perspective] "is not intended to displace or compete with other psychological perspectives, but rather to complement them by framing them in the multicultural contexts in which all psychological interpretation occurs.... (Pedersen 1999, pp. 13-14)

Ethics in a Multicultural Context

According to Berry et al. (1992), ethics are guided by one of three general perspectives: relativism, absolutism, and universalism:

- The relativist [ethical] position avoids imposing value judgments and allows each cultural context to be understood in its own terms ...
- The absolutist [ethical] position disregards problems of ethnocentrism and applies the same evaluative criteria across cultures in the same fixed and unchanging perspective, ... [or]
- The universalist [ethical] position assumes that while psychological processes, such as pleasure and pain, might be the same in all cultures, the way they are manifested is significantly different in each culture.... (pp. 225-226)

Pederson (1995a) takes the position that

> Ethical principles generated in one cultural context cannot be applied to other substantially different cultural contexts without modification.... However, before making any modification the counselor must distinguish between 'fundamental' ethical principles that are not negotiable and 'discretionary' aspects that can be modified and adapted to each setting. If the fundamental principles are compromised, the result is relativism: justice determined by whatever the common practice of a community might be. If the discretionary aspects are not modified, the result is an absolutist domination by special interest groups that benefit from the status quo. (quoted in Pedersen 1997, pp. 224-225).

Some Ethical Principles for Multicultural Practice:

1. The acknowledgment and valuation of diversity, in terms of understanding how race, culture, and ethnicity contribute to the uniqueness of each individual, family, and community, as well as how diversity exists within each ethnic, cultural, and racial group,
2. The importance of each clinician's cultural self-assessment in regard to his or her own culture and its impact on personal and professional beliefs and behaviors,
3. The obligation to systematically acquire of cultural awareness of each client's background, and
4. The adaptation of skills to the needs and styles of each client's culture (Rounds et al. 1994, as cited in Mishne 2002, p. x).

The American Psychological Association (1993) Code of Ethics provides a sociocultural framework that specifies the core abilities essential to ethical decision making:

- understanding how culture shapes behavior
- recognizing cultural diversity
- understanding the socioeconomic and psychological roles of culture
- understanding how socioeconomic and political factors influence cultural groups
- achieving self-awareness of one's own sociocultural identity.

But despite the current widespread movement toward multiculturalism, there is one significant caveat that is most clearly stated by bell hooks (1995):

> The most recent effort to undermine progressive bonding between people of color is the institutionalization of 'multiculturalism' [because it encourages ethnic grouping and competition between groups.] [What we need is a] progressive politics of solidarity that embraces... (1) a broad-based identity politics which acknowledges specific cultural and ethnic legacies, histories, etc. ...[while] (2) it simultaneously promotes ... an inclusive understanding of what is gained when people of color unite to resist white supremacy.... [This] is the only way to ensure that multicultural democracy will become a reality. (p. 203)

With these preliminary considerations regarding multiculturalism as a movement and the importance for considering ethics multiculturally, let us now consider ten different perspectives for illuminating various aspects of multicultural concerns.

Perspective 1: Five Dimensions of Culture

From extensive cross-cultural research extending over nearly forty years and involving more than eighty countries, Dutch researcher Gert Hofstede (2001) and his many research collaborators have located five basic dimensions of culture along which value systems affect how people think, feel, and act. "I treat culture as the collective programming of the mind that distinguishes the members of one group or category of people from another" (p. 3). "... [P]eople carry 'mental pro-grams' that are developed in the family in early childhood and reinforced in schools and organizations, and these mental programs contain a component of national culture. They are most clearly expressed in the different values that predominate among people from different countries" (pp. xix-xx).

Hofstede's Essential Ingredients of Culture

"From the many terms used to describe visible manifestations of culture, the following three, together with values, cover the total concept rather neatly: symbols, heroes, and rituals....

(1) "Symbols are words, gestures, pictures, and objects that carry often complex meanings recognized as such only by those who share the culture....

(2) "Heroes are persons, alive or dead, real or imaginary, who possess characteristics that are highly prized in a culture and thus serve as models for behavior....

(3) "Rituals are collective activities that are technically unnecessary to the achievement of desired ends, but that within a culture are considered socially essential" (p. 3). *Symbols, heroes, and rituals express the values of each culture.*

Hofstede's Five Cultural Dimensions

1. **Power distance** is the extent to which the less powerful members of organizations and institutions accept and expect that power is distributed unequally. The basic problem involved is the degree of human inequality that underlies the functioning of each particular society.

2. **Uncertainly avoidance** is the extent to which a culture programs its members to feel either uncomfortable or comfortable in unstructured situations. Unstructured situations are novel, unknown, surprising, different from usual. The basic problem involved is the degree to which a society tries to control the uncontrollable.

3. **Individualism versus collectivism** is the degree to which individuals are supposed to look after themselves or remain integrated into groups, usually around the family. Positioning itself between [the individual and the collective] poles is a very basic problem all societies face.

4. **Masculinity versus femininity**, refers to the distribution of emotional roles between the genders, which is another

31

fundamental problem for any society to which a range of solutions are found; it opposes "tough" masculine to "tender" feminine societies [though concrete gender roles may not be the same as the tough-tender dichotomy].

5. **Long-term versus short-term orientation** refers to the extent to which a culture programs its members to accept delayed gratification of their material, social, and emotional needs.

Hofstede believes that dilemmas in cross-cultural communications need to be considered in light of how members from participating cultures experience each of these universal dimensions. His massive cross-cultural research places cultural values from more than the eighty nations studied in relation to each other. His goal is to highlight how complex intercultural communication truly is:

> I believe that the battle for the recognition of the cultural component in our ideas is worth fighting. More so now than one or two generations ago, most of us meet people with cultural backgrounds different from our own and are expected to work with them. If we maintain the naive assumption that because they look like us they also think like us, our joint efforts will not get very far. If we begin to realize that our own ideas are culturally limited, from that moment we need the others, we can never be self-sufficient again. Only others with different mental programs can help us find the limitations of our own. Once we have realized we are blind persons in front of the elephant, we start to welcome the exchange with other blind persons. Changes take decades, if not centuries. If the inheritance of the Roman Empire still separates Belgium from the Netherlands, two countries in intimate contact for more than 2,000 years, we should not expect that anyone can change the minds of Serbs, Russians, or

Albanians within a few years. In organizing our world, we had better take mental programs as given facts. A popular business slogan is 'Think globally, act locally.' To me this phrase is both naive and arrogant. No one...can think globally. We all think according to our own local software. What intercultural encounters are about is recognizing that we think differently but resolving our common problems anyway. The slogan should be 'Think locally, act globally.'" (pp. 453-454)

Perspective 2: The Mimetic Evolution of Culture

Biologist Susan Blackmore in her book *The Meme Machine* (1999) integrates several decades of research into the evolution of "memes," the cultural replicators that parallel genes. Her ideas about memes are important in cross-cultural encounters because the power of imitation guides all of our thoughts, feelings, and behaviors.

> 'For more than three thousand million years, DNA has been the only replicator worth talking about in the world. But it does not necessarily hold these monopoly rights for all time. Whenever conditions arise in which a new kind of replicator *can* make copies of itself, the new replicators *will* tend to take over, and start a new kind of evolution of their own....' [Dawkins 1976] Of course, memes could only come into existence when the genes had provided brains that were capable of imitation—and the nature of those brains must have influenced which memes took hold and which did not. However, once memes had come into existence they

would be expected to take on a life of their own.... (pp. 30-31)

From the early days of Darwinism analogies have been drawn between biological evolution and the evolution of culture.... In some ways it is obvious that ideas and cultures evolve—that is, changes are gradual and build on what went before. Ideas spread from one place to another and from one person to another (Sperber 1990). Inventions do not spring out of nowhere but depend on previous inventions, and so on. However, truly Darwinian explanations require more than just the idea of accumulating changes over time.... The whole point of a memetic theory of cultural evolution is to treat memes as replicators in their own right. This means that memetic selection drives the evolution of ideas in the interests of replicating the memes, not the genes.... (p. 24)

In memetic terms, all that happens—whether in science or art—is selective imitation. The emotions, the intellectual struggles, the subjective experiences—these are all parts of the complex system that leads to some behaviours being imitated and others not. And it is because imitation lets loose a second replicator that ideas begin to 'have a life of their own.' (p. 29)

For Blackmore, as for Dawkins and Dennett, memetic evolution means that people are different. Their ability to imitate creates a second replicator that acts in its own interests and can produce behaviour that is memetically adaptive but biologically maladaptive. Considering memes as second-level replicators whose job, like DNA, is simply to keep replicating allows us to understand why so many cultural oddities exist all over the planet. All primates are imitators. Humans have taken imitation to abstract levels of values, symbols, heroes, and rituals. Once a thought, feeling, or behavior is imitated, it can easily, blindly, and militantly perpetuate itself for any of a myriad of reasons.

Cultures evolve based on selective mimetics over long periods of time in specific ethnic contexts. Individuals are born into complex mimetic networks, which, like complex language networks, are gradually acquired over long periods of time through daily immersion in a web of relationships. Thoughts, feelings, and behavior acquired in mimetic networks are highly resistant to change because human imitation has served to construct living human realities. We have all been "carefully taught" to live within the limits of reality and this includes the limits of our culturally- and ethnically-constructed mimetic realities.

This means that a counselor, therapist or educator trying to understand an idea, practice, ritual, or value in the mimetic soup of another is inevitably bound to fail in many regards. As professionals then, simply understanding cultural and ethnic variation cannot be our goal. Rather, we must ask ourselves how we can best position ourselves so that those who live in other mimetic systems can begin to represent, elaborate, and achieve their own understandings of what they are thinking, feeling, or doing themselves in their own life contexts.

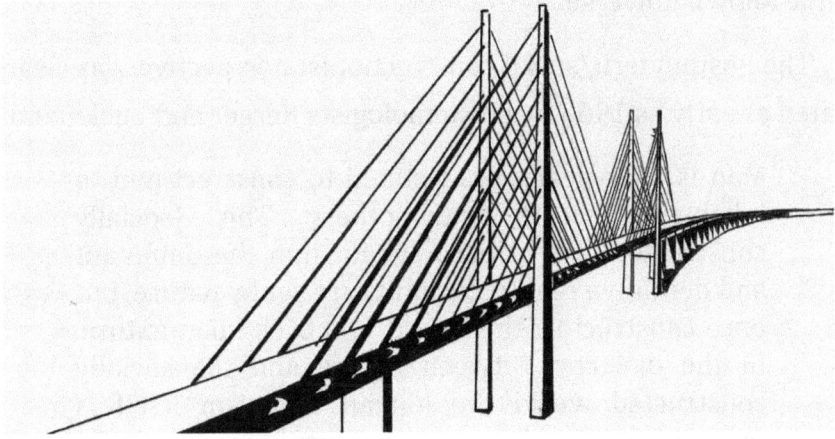

Perspective 3: Postmodern/Social Constructionism

Galileo with his telescope, Newton with his falling apple, and Einstein with his space-time relativity have all led us through the twentieth century with the hope of discovering finally the grand unified laws of the natural or God-given universe around us. This so-called "modern" attitude toward truth, certainty, and reality holds that there will come a moment in human history when the great mysteries of the universe will be ours to behold with clarity once and for all.

Early sociologists, anthropologists, and psychologists once held the modernist view that the truths of human nature would someday become objectively and definitively understood. That was before the incredible diversity and complexity of human culture and ethnicity began to become understood. This so-called "modern" hope of ultimately knowing everything has faltered seriously in light of what we have learned over the past century—mainly, that there are many contrasting, competing, and even conflicting ways to view and to interact with the infinite realities of the known universe.

The Postmodern/social constructionist perspective was clearly stated as early as 1966 by epistemologists Berger and Luckmann.

> Man is biologically predestined to construct and to inhabit a world with others. This [socially constructed] world becomes for him the dominant and definitive reality. Its limits are set by nature, but once constructed, this world acts back upon nature. In the dialectic between nature and the socially constructed world the human organism itself is transformed. In this same dialectic man produces reality and thereby produces himself. (p. 183)

Thus "modern" is the common-sense attitude that objectively true certainties can ultimately be discovered and controlled, while "Postmodern" is the attitude that all knowledge is a product of various kinds of perspectives and subjective constructions—individual and collective. In Postmodern, social constructionist thinking, while we may no longer be able to know things with certainty, we can certainly generate interesting and useful perspectives from which to view, interpret, and interact with all realities that we do encounter. The Postmodern constructionist view is that we are forever limited to defining certain vantage points, operational definitions, and perspectives that aid us in focusing our curiosity, collecting data, and formulating ideas— *theories about what our observations mean to us rather than theories about how things really are.*

Implications of Postmodern Constructionism for Professionals

The Postmodern constructionist search to understand human culture involves the study of an infinite array of personal meanings as they become enacted and understood in dynamic relationships, not in finally unearthing the biological, anthropological, or psychological truths about human nature cross-culturally viewed. That is, in exploring the many complex, affective, and interpersonal aspects of anyone's cultural and/or ethnic orientations, professionals must be able to do more than simply explore the behavior and personal narratives put before them. Rather, through the interpersonal engagement of the therapeutic relationship itself, the client and the professional have the possibility of (1) co-constructing new more encompassing interpersonal narratives; (2) engaging in novel interpersonal encounters; and (3) mutually creating fresh meanings of their experiences of culture and ethnicity (Gergen, 1994; Hoffman, 1998; D. B. Stern, 1997).

The Postmodern social constructionist perspective allows us to consider how cultural constructions create cultural and ethnic realities that become internalized early in life and manifest as transference and countertransference phenomena that later appear in counseling, psychotherapy, and educational settings.

Perspective 4: Ethnicity and Sexuality

From multicultural studies comes a newly emerging awareness about "the power of sex to shape ideas and feelings about race, ethnicity, and the nation and how sexual images, fears, and desires shape racial, ethnic and national stereotypes, differences, and conflicts...how sex matters insinuate themselves into all things racial, ethnic, and national...[and] how ethnic boundaries are also sexual boundaries" (Joane Nagel 2003, p. 1).

> Differences of color, culture, country, ancestry, language, and religion are the materials out of which ethnic, racial, and national identities and boundaries are built. Ethnicity and sexuality join together to form a barrier to hold some people in and keep others out, to define who is pure and who is impure, to shape our view of ourselves and others, to fashion feelings of sexual desire and notions of sexual desirability, to provide us with seemingly 'natural' sexual preferences for some partners and 'intuitive' aversions to others, to leave us with a taste for some

ethnic sexual encounters and a distaste for others. Ethnicity and sexuality blend together to form sexualized perimeters around ethnic, racial, and national spaces. (ibid.)

Currently developing cross-cultural studies are demonstrating how ethnic and sexual boundaries converge to mark the edges of what are being called ethno-sexual frontiers. Ethonosexual frontiers are constituted not only by ethnic identity variations, but also sexual identity variations, as well as the interactions between ethnic and sexual identities. Ethnosexual connections exist in:

- Artistic depictions of men and women of various ethnicities
- Fears and fantasies implicit in racial stereotypes
- Rules for contact between ethnic groups
- Men's and women's places in different societies
- Ethnic attitudes toward desire and disgust
- Beliefs regarding characteristics and potencies of ethnic and immigrant peoples
- Appetites and aversions toward ethnic individuals
- Sexual overtones in ethnic cleansing, genocide, and war efforts.

As an example of the way sexual ideologies construct ethnic others as inferior to the accepted norm—i.e., as oversexed, undersexed, perverted, or dangerous, Judith Halberstam's research has shown that currently in the United States dominant white middle-class ideas about acceptable masculinity and male sexuality define African-American and Latino men as excessively masculine and over-sexed and Asian men as insufficiently masculine or undersexed (Halberstam, 1998).

Another example from multicultural studies reveals how boundaries are universally maintained by ethnic groups in the tendency to construct "our group" as vigorous (usually our men) and pure (usually our women). While "those others" are generally constructed as sexually depraved (usually their men) and promiscuous (usually their women) (Nagel, p. 10).

Ethnosexual boundaries often constitute exotic destinations and erotic locations that are surveilled and supervised, policed and patrolled, regulated and restricted from both sides, but whose boundaries nevertheless are constantly being transversed by individuals seeking links with stimulating ethnic Otherness. Nagel's work defines various kinds of ethnosexual adventurers, sojourners, settlers, and invaders. She researches the worldwide sex industry created by multinational military operations and international tourism, an industry that appeals to the erotic excitement of the ethnosexual frontier. She cites the Internet as offering the latest titillating adventures in ethnosexual encounters. Researchers in ethnosexual history are now suggesting that the primary binary in human thought—whether in families, clans, tribes, religious, or ethnic and national groups—is between Us and Them, not between male and female. That is, that gender identities are secondary to and participate in constructing in- and out-group identities.

The listening perspective that links ethnicity and sexuality views sex as a core constitutive element of race, ethnicity, and the nation; and that race, ethnicity and nationalism are crucial components of sexual and moral boundaries and systems. In counseling, psychotherapy, and education beyond what is consciously and explicitly presented, client and professional have the additional task of being alert to how many different kinds of ethnicity and sexuality are embedded in each of their conscious and unconscious histories, and how in the therapeutic relationship itself new erotics are continuously being mutually co-constructed based on the ethnic and sexuality dimensions both participants bring to the relationship. We can no longer simply take anyone's stated cultural, ethnic, or sexual orientations or gender identities at face value in personal or professional life.

Perspective 5:
Issues in Urban Life—Poverty, Adversity, Immigration, Exposure to Racism, and PTSD

Poverty

While poverty, adversity, racism, and immigration are by no means unique to inner city living, these themes have received the most attention in the central city. Most clinicians and educators have little training or experience in dealing directly with these issues. Urban life, poverty, and immigration are here to stay and this is the last frontier for overt prejudice and racism. How can we as professionals attune ourselves to the socio-cultural problems faced by the impoverished, the displaced, the hated? How can we as professionals aid in

- promoting positive social mirroring
- eliminating symbolic violence
- preventing internalized negativity before it takes over

- harnessing the human resource that immigrants, the inner-city poor, and their children represent?

"Life in the inner city entails a greater burden of stress, loss, and trauma than life in working-class-and-up communities. These conditions predispose to psychopathology (Brown and Harris, 1978) and to complications in parenting young children (Halpern, 1993). [Urban conditions] form part of what is enacted and experienced in the transference and countertransference when one works (psychologically) with inner-city patients" (Altman 1995, p. 1).

"Adversity can also breed uncommon strength, as documented in the studies of 'resilient' children (Anthony and Cohler, 1987; Neiman, 1987). Inner-city people may also be buffered from the effects of stress in certain ways unavailable to other people. Inner-city people may bring to the therapy situation great resources, as well as expectations of a healing relationship that may be unfamiliar to the middle-class North American mental-health professional" (Altman, p. 2).

Immigration

"In [most] original home environments, immigrant and refugee children and families had quite functional cultural values and practices that operated as strengths and bound them to their countrymen. But in journeying to a new host country, many of these cultural values have been reevaluated, because the receiving country's culture either fails to understand them or disagrees with their priority" (Fong 2004, p. 3).

"Many immigrant families encourage their children to pick up certain cultural competencies (such as the English language) while fiercely resisting others. They come to see certain American attitudes and behaviors as a threat to family unity" (Suárez-Orozco & Suárez-Orozco 2001, p. 79).

"Although poverty is a common concern, immigrants and refugees regularly experience other economically-related problems, as well. Underemployment for immigrants from professional classes, or joblessness, is particularly worrisome for men. For women, the economic problems depend on their own employability, and children are affected if they have to sacrifice childhood and studies to add to the family income" (Fong, p. 1).

> After taking care of the essential needs, immigrants will begin to confront some unanticipated realities. Many will experience a variety of psychological problems. Most frequently, the cumulative losses of loved ones and familiar contexts will lead to a range of feelings, from mild sadness to depression to 'perpetual mourning'. For others, the general dissonance in cultural expectations and the loss of predictable context will be experienced as anxiety and an acute disorientation. Many immigrants who arrive with exaggerated expectations of opportunity and wealth must come to terms with a starker reality. Rather than face a 'relatively uniform mainstream' culture, immigrants today must navigate the complex currents of what we call a 'culture of multiculturalism'... [that shapes] the experiences, perceptions, and behavioral repertoires of immigrants.... An outcome of our culture of multiculturalism is that new immigrants are pushed to be socialized into becoming [e.g.] 'Latino' or 'Asian' [rather than being allowed to identify with their culture of origin]. (Suárez-Orozco & Suárez-Orozco 2001, pp. 62-65).

"The problems for the immigrant children seem to be affected by variables such as the parents' status, the journey to the United States, and the age and gender of the child. Children who are undocumented may have problems with identity, play relationships, and age-appropriate social skills. Many undocumented children report that they feel constantly 'hunted.' The parents may severely constrict their activities outside the home for fear that they will be apprehended. It is frightening to anticipate that their children may be detained at any time. For children with undocumented parents, there is also the fear that the parent will be caught and deported. A common terror many undocumented children experience is that they will never be reunited with their parent. "In some cases, the undocumented child may unconsciously become the family's 'scapegoat; while the documented child may occupy the role of 'the golden child.' This imbalance creates tensions and resentments." (Suárez-Orozco & Suárez-Orozco 2001, pp. 34-35).

Post-Traumatic Stress

The sequelae of trauma (van der Kolk 1987), posttraumatic stress disorders and dissociative disorders are also widespread and transmitted from generation to generation, as is child maltreatment (Lyons-Ruth & Zeanah 1993). When these people—adults, parents, children—enter our offices, they enter with the full range of transference expectations born of trauma. The analyst must expect, in the transference, to take on the role of rescuer, victim, abuser, and neglectful parent, in the ways Davies and Frawley (1992) and Gabbard (1992) have shown to occur in the analysis of adult survivors of childhood sexual abuse (Altman 1995, pp. 1-2).

Cultural Mentors

"A charismatic mentor can ... play a decisive role. We have seen how a caring baseball coach who explicitly instructs his Dominican protégés in the "rules of the game" (both in the field and in life) made an immense difference in the careers of his immigrant students." (Altman 1995, pp. 152-153) Albert Camus, himself an immigrant to Algeria, wrote to his teacher Monsieur Germain: "I have just been given far too great an honor, one I neither sought nor solicited. But when I heard the news [of having won the Nobel Prize], my first thought, after my mother, was of you. Without you, without the affectionate hand you extended to the small poor child that I was, without your teaching, and your example, none of this would have happened. This sort of honor...gives me an opportunity to tell you what you have been and still are for me, and to assure you that your efforts, your work, and the generous heart you put into it still live in one of your little schoolboys who, despite the years, has never stopped being your grateful pupil. I embrace you with all my heart" (quoted in Altman 1995, p. 153).

Summary

Today there are clear and unequivocal advantages to being able to operate in multiple cultural codes—as anyone working in a major (and now not-so-major) corporation knows. There are social, economic, cognitive, and aesthetic advantages to being able to transverse cultural spaces. "Immigrant children are poised to maximize that unique advantage. While many view these children's cultural—including linguistic—skills as a threat, we see them as precious assets to be cultivated" (Altman 1995, p. 160). Urban conditions can be grim but with help many can transcend early trauma and learn to live fulfilling lives.

Perspective 6:
Ghosts: Individual, Positional and Transgenerational Internalizations

The great psychological controversy of the nineteenth century concerned which was more important in human development, nature or nurture? Sigmund Freud believed that his most significant discovery was that more important than either nature or nurture in human beings was a third force: the progressive elaboration from birth of an "internal world." Each stage of our emotional-relational development is molded not only by the genetic and constitutional load we bring into the world with us, but by how we experience and construct in memory each unfolding interpersonal encounter. We may joke about perceiving the proverbial glass as half-empty or half-full, but at some level we know that our early character formation influences all of our subsequent perceptions and projections. We construct ongoing subjective worlds based on how we have experienced relationships in the past.

The central concept of psychotherapy is "transference"—by whatever name we choose to call it. Transference of internalized emotional patterns of relating operates in all relationships but is particularly noticeable in trust relationships. Countertransference is the term applied to the professional's transferred emotional relatedness patterns. Psychotherapy teaches us that we all carry within us transference ghosts from the past that influence how we live our present relationships. That is, the central assumption of psychotherapy is that early conditioning in the context of emotionally significant relationships and dynamically impactful experiences heavily influence the ways we construct our subsequent perceptions and lives. The theories and practices of psychotherapy, as well as contemporary neuroscience (see LeDoux 1996, 2002; Edelman 1993, 2006, 2000 (with Tononi); Damasio 1994, 1999, 2003; Pert 1997; Lewis et al. 2000; Cozolino 2002; and Siegal 1999, 2007) support our professional belief that in emotionally significant relationships later in life, people can learn to focus on and to alter their relational patterns and behaviors.

Three Kinds of Ghosts Inhabit Our Internal Worlds:

- **An individual internalization** would be a way we each organize our perceptions and projections based on emotionally significant experience from our personal and familial past—such as abuse, trauma, success, or privilege.

- **A positional internalization** refers to a way we may psychologically organize our experience based upon some condition of the socio-cultural position we were born into or came to occupy—for example, social class or racial prejudice; gender or sexuality bias; or handicapped, immigrant, or refugee status.[2]

- **A transgenerational internalization** is a psychological organization or orientation based upon experiences our parents or ancestors may have suffered but that persists in haunting our present—for example, the possibility of poor self-esteem carried by an African-American individual based upon generations of maltreatment.

Attitudes of ethnic or racial superiority, supremacy, or privilege are further examples of transgenerational transmission or haunting. Racial hatred, religious intolerance, class prejudice, and white guilt are all sustained through internalization and transgenerational transmission.

In 1975 Nicolas Abraham introduced the concept of the "transgenerational phantom" moving the focus of psychodynamic psychotherapy beyond the individual because it postulates that some people unwittingly inherit the secret 'psychic substance' of their ancestors' lives.

> The terms 'phantom,' 'ghosts,' and 'revenants' as used by Abraham and Torok, derive from folklore giving psychological substance to age-old beliefs..., according to which only certain categories of the dead return to torment the living: those who were denied the rite of burial or died an unnatural, abnormal death, were criminals or outcasts, or suffered injustice in their lifetime... .In Abraham's view, the dead do not return, but their lives'

---

[2] Maher and Tetreault (1996) define positionality as suggesting "that rather than being composed of any fixed 'essence' or individual identity, we all develop amid networks of relationships that themselves can be explored, analyzed, and changed, as long as people understand that they are not simply individuals, but differentially placed members of an unequal social order" (p. 163).

unfinished business is unconsciously handed down to their descendants. Laying the dead to rest and cultivating our ancestors implies uncovering their shameful secrets, understanding their nameless and undisclosed suffering.... [U]nsuspected, the dead continue to lead a devastating psychic half-life in us. (N. Rand, quoted in Abraham & Tarok 1994, pp. 166-167)

Ghosts in Counseling, Psychotherapy, and Education

The special difficulty of [therapeutic work with transgenerational phantoms] lies in the patient's horror at violating a parent's or a family's guarded secret, even though the secret's text and content are inscribed within the patient's own unconscious. The horror of transgression, in the strict sense of the term, is compounded by the risk of undermining the fictitious yet necessary integrity of the parental figure in question.

Recent attachment research clearly demonstrates the operation of transgenerational phantoms in the mechanisms of biologically based and psychologically mediated human attachment. Says Marone (1998):

> Parental functions are organized by the parents' representational systems, defenses, and strategies, and their manifestation through family scripts, which in turn were formed under the influence of their own parents' representational systems. There is now ample and robust empirical support for this hypothesis. Identification with negative and or abusive aspects of the parents plays an important role in intergenerational transmission of disturbance. (pp. 135-139)

As a clear example of how transgenerational haunting operates, in her book, *Killing Rage: Ending Racism*, bell hooks (1995) raises questions about

> negative habits of being that may have emerged as forms of political resistance ... in the days of extreme racial apartheid. For example, dissimulation—the practice of taking on any appearance needed to manipulate a situation—is a form of masking that black folks have historically used to survive in white supremacist settings. As a social practice, [dissimulation] promoted duplicity, the wearing of masks, hiding true feelings and intent. While this may have been useful in daily relations with all-powerful white exploiters and oppressors...as a paradigm for social relations it has undermined bonds of love and intimacy." Only as African-Americans break with the culture of shame that has demanded that we be silent about our pain will we be able to engage holistic strategies for healing that will break this cycle." (pp. 143-144)

Psychoanalyst Vamik Volkan (2004) writes:

> There is far more to this transgenerational transmission of massive trauma than children mimicking the behavior of parents or hearing stories of the event told by the older generation. Rather, it is the end result of mostly unconscious psychological processes by which survivors deposit into their progeny's core identities their own injured self-images in order to gain relief from feelings of shame and humiliation, the inability to be assertive, and the inability to mourn. A Holocaust survivor, for example, deposits his or her image of him or herself as a damaged person into the developing personal identity of his or her child; thus, the parent's self-image 'lives on' in the child. Then the parent

unconsciously assigns to the image of him or herself that is now in the child specific tasks of reparation that rightfully belong to the survivor: [such as] to reverse shame and humiliation, to turn passivity into activity, to tame the sense of aggression, and to mourn the losses associated with the trauma. What is passed to the offspring is not the traumatized person's memories of the event, then, for memory can belong only to the survivor of trauma and cannot be transmitted; deposited parental self-images are the only elements by which the representation of traumatic history can be passed from person to person." (pp. 48-49)

Implications for Counseling, Psychotherapy, and Education

Cross-cultural research in attachment, neuroscience, and infant intersubjectivity confirms that individual, positional, and transgenerational phantoms inhabit our inner worlds, informing us who we are and how we are to be in our relationships and in the world. People raised in different socio-political, economic, and cultural circumstances experience their ghosts differently. Counseling, psychotherapy, and educational settings provide an opportunity to represent in symbols, language, and enactments the phantoms that inhabit our inner worlds. The task of the facilitating professional cannot be to have a knowledge of all of the types of personal, familial, and cultural haunting that diverse people experience. But rather to co-create with the client a setting that is maximally conducive to the emergence of internal representations in symbols, words, and actions. Phantoms cannot survive exposure to the light of day!

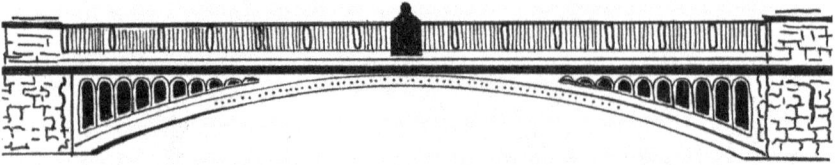

Perspective 7:
Difference, Hatred, and Discrimination

Emerging Themes Regarding Difference

We now know that:

- Dominance/submission hierarchies throughout the world still largely remain structured by gender and skin-color differences.

- Gender, sexuality, race, culture, ethnicity, social class, able-bodiedness, dominance strivings, and privilege remain linked in a complex political, economic, social, and psychological network of global structures.

- Overt, legally sanctioned forms of discrimination have slowly given way in this country to covert, inadvertent, and unconscious forms of discrimination.

- Hatred of difference, of perceived otherness, has many sources in human life, but it is ultimately thought to arise from primary mental processes that precede even the recognition of gender

- Hatred of difference in human life evolves as a way of "WE" establishing consensual (social group) knowledge and power in the face of perennial individual "I" uncertainty, helplessness, and insecurity—i.e., of turning passivity into activity. (Moss 2004)

This last point merits elaboration. In a recent book edited by Donald Moss, *Hatred in the First Person Plural: Psychoanalytic Essays on Racism, Homophobia, Misogyny, and Terror*, twelve psychoanalysts who are each research experts in some form of prejudice write essays from their special vantage points on how hatred operates in the WE of their specialty. In Moss's introductory essay that orients the book he notes how we are each born into the world as uncertain and insecure beings. If our early environment is adequately supportive, we learn to navigate fear, uncertainty, and insecurity to form an active, alive, and basically secure sense of self—an "I" who loves and respects others. However, with inadequate early environmental support people fail to overcome their primitive insecurities, and uncertainties, leaving them perennially vulnerable to fear in social settings. Such people cannot rely on a secure sense of I to get them through safely and so learn to identify with the powerful WE of group prejudice. "We know how women are. We can't trust them. We hate them." Or, "We know how blacks [homosexuals, Puerto Ricans, whites, Catholics, etc.] are. They are inferior to us. They do strange things and think strange ways. WE hate them." Considering personal insecurity leading to identity formation with prejudicial ideas adds substantially to our understanding various forms of bigotry.

Considerations Regarding "Race" and Racism

Two centuries ago, Carl Linnaeus classified homo sapiens into four races based on (visibly observable,) phenotypic traits. Since then, other taxonomists have argued for as few as three and as many as thirty-seven races (Molnar 1992). The postmodern approach considers "race as a category derived from the conceptual and language network in which it is embedded. This network gives us our categories for classifying and understanding people, including ourselves" (Altman 1995, p. 69). "Mindful of World War II, UNESCO worked to debunk the idea of race as a biological fact so that it could never again be used to support aggression and genocide" (Yee et al. 1993, p. 1132, quoted in Pedersen 1997, p. 48).

"This also holds for red, brown, and yellow peoples. For one generation—thirty-five years—we have embarked on a multiracial democracy with significant breakthroughs and glaring silences" (West, (1993/2001, p. xiv).

Racism, as defined by Kinlock (1974), is an uncritical acceptance of a negative social definition of a group identified as a race on perceived physical grounds along with the (socially condoned) legitimacy of the discriminating treatment accompanying that definition. "Covert, unintentional racism is a form of racism that comes about because of laws or traditions that are racist in nature, but the protagonist is unaware of the racist roots [or implications] of these laws or traditions" (Mio and Awakuni 2000, p. 21).

Charles Ridley (1995) writes:

> Unintentional behavior is perhaps the most insidious form of racism. Unintentional racists are unaware of the harmful consequences of their behavior. They may be well-intentioned, and on the surface, their behavior may appear to be responsible. Because individuals, groups, or

institutions that engage in unintentional racism do not wish to do harm, it is difficult to get them to see themselves as racist. They are more likely to deny their racism. [For example, W]hite reporters are continually referring to political violence between factions of Blacks as 'Black-on-Black violence.' However, whenever there was a clash between supporters of the Irish Republican Army and the Ulster Unionists in Northern Ireland, I did not hear one international correspondent refer to it as White-on-White violence.... The entire war in Bosnia-Herzegovina was between White ethnic Europeans, yet again, no reference to it as White-on-White violence could be heard in the international press. Were these reporters blatantly racist? I would suspect not. However, their reporting certainly reflected covert, unintentional racism.... (pp. 22-30)

Another aspect of covert, unintentional racism involves acts of omission as opposed to acts of commission. People experience crime as a ethnic minority issue because the media reports things like 'Black gang violence,' 'Latino gang violence,' and 'Asian gang violence'...." Such reports do not protect the larger African-American, Latino, and Asian communities from suspicion. Whenever Whites are involved in gang activities, they are characterized as 'The Mafia' or 'White supremacists,' thus allowing the average White citizen to be protected from incrimination, safe in the knowledge that he or she is not in the Mafia or involved with the White supremacist movement." (p. 30)

bell hooks (1995) writes on the African-American Identity Crisis:

Mass media's trivialization of black rage reinforces white denial that white supremacy exists, that it is institutionalized, perpetuated by a system that condones the dehumanization of black people, by encouraging everyone to dismiss rage against racism as in no way a response to concrete reality since the black folks they see complaining are affluent…. (p. 29)

"When the discourse of blackness is in no way connected to an effort to promote collective black self-determination it becomes simply another resource appropriated by the colonizer. It is then possible for white supremacist culture to be perpetuated and maintained even as it appears to be more welcoming, more inclusive" (hooks, 1995, p. 178).

"The contemporary crisis of identity is best resolved by our collective willingness as African-Americans to acknowledge that there is no monolithic black community, no normative black identity. There is a shared history that frames the construction of our diverse black experiences. Knowledge of that history is needed by everyone as we seek to construct self and identity." (p. 247)

Race and Ethnicity in Counseling, Psychotherapy, and Education

Says psychoanalyst Kimberlyn Leary (1997):

When I open the door to the waiting room to greet a new patient, that I am obviously a person of color constitutes an implicit and important self-disclosure. At the present moment in time, racial similarity or difference in the consulting room immediately implicates us into a cultural conversation and one about which it is difficult to talk openly…. With most patients, if racial similarity or, more typically, racial difference is not mentioned at some point during an evaluation or during the first month of a treatment, I typically comment on the fact that the patient hasn't mentioned it directly. I might, for example, acknowledge the social climate surrounding open talk about race in this country ... In this way, I am offering the patient an opportunity to consider the expanded possibilities for communication offered in treatment. (pp. 419-421)

Holmes (1992) comments on the regularly occurring transference fear in a cross-race treatment dyad that she or he will express aggressive urges in racist attitudes. She also discusses the wish that race will not come up in the content of the therapy session—or that if it does, that it will not be interpreted.

Simpson (1993) suggests that therapists also fear that their countertransference will be coded in racial terms. This is also a fear of counselors and educators. He further notes that it is "strange that those of us who are prepared to accept our murderous wishes, for example, towards members of our families cannot, or will not, accept that we might have 'racist' thoughts or feelings" (p. 291).

Says Leary (1997), "It seems inevitable that all of us—patients and analysts—will have racial thoughts and feelings that are libidinally and aggressively tinged. Speaking to the patient's concerns about racist content and the sociocultural realities of race can become a way of understanding the patient's relationship to his/her own mind [and the racial transference and countertransference, as well]" (p. 420).

Psychologist Pratyusha Tummala-Nara examined the research bearing on the relevance of skin color in the intrapsychic as well as in the interpersonal processes of clients and therapists. She concludes that in most cultures throughout the world power and domination are associated with a light skin color. "Preference for light skin divides and shapes identity and experience within various ethic communities; it has a significant impact on psychological adjustment and contributes to an increased understanding of the experiences of ethnic minorities; it perpetuates the myth of lower capacities for people of color and contributes to divisions within ethnic groups" (cited in Morris 2005, p. 59).

Since speaking of skin color may be considered politically incorrect in different therapist/client or student/educator ethnic combinations, significant aspects of personal identity development, as well as interpersonal relationship development, are in danger of remaining unaddressed in therapy (Tummala-Nara, cited ibid., p. 60).

Deaf People as a Minority Culture

Deafness is widely considered a physical handicap and so the culture that deaf people have developed over time has gone largely unnoticed. According to Backenroth-Ohsako (1999),

> Today, deaf people are demanding to be recognized as a cultural and linguistic minority group ... The Deaf community has had a more difficult time overcoming inferiority stereotyping by the majority culture than other minority groups, since deaf people have been viewed as a disability group.... The multicultural mosaic model can best be applied in today's society, since interaction between deaf and hearing people is facilitated by mediating deaf individuals having cultural competence in both the Deaf community and the hearing dominant society. (pp. 111-112)
>
> Thus there has been a shift from a clinical-pathological view of deafness to a cultural view of

deafness, and the deaf have been 'seen as a cultural and linguistic minority group within a multicultural society' (Gregory 1992, p. 184). (p. 139)

Jewish Difference

In contemporary culture, Jewish identity as a marker of difference is largely ignored or made invisible, a fact that is particularly striking given the large number of Jews working in the therapy, counseling, and educational fields (Beck 1991a; Siegel & Cole 1991). "This omission is a reflection of a pervasive attitude within the larger society, that Jewish identity and anti-Jewish oppression are nonissues in the world today" (Beck et al. 2003, p. 237).

"In the United States today, Jews are primarily regarded as a religious group. However, Jewish identity also includes a sense of belonging to the Jewish people (in addition to whatever national citizenship one might have); thus there is a Jewish historical and cultural identity or ethnicity even for those who reject religion altogether. Institutionalized persecutions of Jews have persisted over many centuries, dramatically illustrated by the long history of pogroms and the Nazi Holocaust in Europe. Recent events around the world—for example, in Russia (Bohlen 1999) and Japan (Goodman &. Miyazawa 1995)—provide evidence of ongoing global hatred toward Jews. "Although it is true that institutionalized anti-Semitism in the United States is at an all-time low, anti-Semitism itself within society is not, as evidenced by the proliferation of extremist anti-Semitic tracts and activity (Dees 2000) and recent incidents of violence against Jews (Anti-Defamation League 2002; Dedman 1999; Sterngold 1999).

[Therapists, counselors, and educators] need to learn that it is important to explore signs of low self-esteem or negative self-image in Jewish clients as likely indicators of internalized oppression. Thus, feelings of being unattractive, undesirable, or disliked, or of behaving 'inappropriately,' should be considered as possible reflections of messages about Jews that clients have absorbed from the dominant culture (Brody 1997; Weiner 1990). Another important thing for [professionals] to understand is that, because of their history of persecution, Jews may live in a state of what Schwartz (1995) called chronic terror. Many may feel that being visible as a Jew brings increased risk of threat and harm and that it is not outside the realm of possibility that they will be killed. Although such feelings may not be conscious most of the time, they can be seen in patterns of behavior that suggest ongoing efforts to 'survive.' For example, perfectionism, overcontrol, and obsessive attention to detail carry the implication that one's life depends on hyper-vigilance about every aspect. Overwork and overachievement can be viewed as desperate efforts by Jews to maintain a place in organizations or professions that are all too ready to exclude them. The controlling and intrusive parenting behaviors often attributed to Jewish mothers can be recognized as originating from this chronic terror, which becomes focused on protecting their children from perceived imminent dangers. (Beck et al., p. 246).

Native-American or First Nation Identity

As sociologist Joanne Nagel (1996) notes,

[O]utside the pale of American race relations [is] a vantage point where race and ethnicity [are] not fixed but changeable, not biologically determined but socially constructed, not constant but situational, not primordial but emergent. From this perspective, Red Power, enacted by Indians (not by Cherokees, Apaches, or Cheyennes each on their own, or even in confederation), [becomes] a puzzle and a challenge. Where [has] this larger 'Indian' identity, organizational network, emergent culture, and activist agenda come from? (p. xii)

"White" colonization of the American continent was marked by persistent westward expansion. "The powerful strategies used in this program of expropriation and subjugation—treaties, wars, removals, reservations—proved to be, quite literally, deadly, especially when combined with the virulence of Old World diseases. The result was the decimation of the North American indigenous population. The number of North American Indians declined from an estimated 2 to 5 million at the time of European contact to fewer than 250,000 at the end of the nineteenth century. Despite differences, there is an overarching sense of "we" (and of "they") that emerges when collective fates and interests are at stake and when the larger group confronts outsiders.... 'Indians' are no more or less real a group than are 'Kurds,' 'Africans,' 'Latinos,' 'Blacks,' or 'Arabs.' (p. 8)

By 1990 the American Indian or First Nation population had grown to 1,878,285. Nagel continues:

The saga of the dramatic twentieth-century rebound in the Indian population and the renaissance of native cultures is not simply a tale of high birth rates or the discovery of forgotten enclaves of native peoples. [But rather] ... 'ethnic renewal'—the process whereby new ethnic identities, communities, and cultures are built or rebuilt out of historical social and symbolic systems.... Through common identification, group formation and reformation, and cultural production and reproduction, ethnicity is revitalized and constantly renewed.... (p. 9)

Red Power [of the 1960s and '70s] was the catalyst that sparked American Indian ethnic renewal. By their own hand, Indian leaders captured the moment and galvanized native and non-native public attention. The resulting Red Power movement prompted a surge in Indian self-identification, promoted a native cultural renaissance, and ultimately prompted a reversal of federal Indian policy. (pp. 12-13)

According to this perspective, an individual's ethnic identity is a composite of the view one has of oneself and the opinions held by others about one's ethnicity.... Ethnic identity lies at the intersection of individual ethnic self-definition (who I am) and collective ethnic attribution (who they say I am).... (p. 21)

Ethnic identity is, then, a dialectic between internal identification and external ascription. It is a socially negotiated and socially constructed status that varies as the audiences permitting particular ethnic options change. As the individual (or group) moves through daily life, ethnic identities are shuffled in and out of prominence depending on the situation. (p. 21)

Allies and Discrimination

Writes Roades and Mio (2000),

In addressing resistance to important social issues, ... we have found that such work is difficult to accomplish without the help of individuals who leave their own demographic group to help those being oppressed. ... There have been allies throughout history—people who work on behalf of others and who take up unpopular causes, people who work on behalf of groups other than their own. There were Whites in the abolition movement who opposed U.S. slavery and worked toward its demise. Christians hid Jews in Europe during World War II, often risking their own lives in the process. Men have marched on behalf of equal rights for women, and heterosexuals continue to support the rights of lesbians and gay men not to be discriminated against in public or private life. (p. 63)

"White people talking to other White people about racism is different from African-Americans or Native-Americans talking to White people about these issues. Men who confront sexism against women in group settings or with other men sound different from women who do the same and are responded to differently. Heterosexuals who label homophobia and work toward equal rights for lesbians and gay men are heard in ways that are seldom possible for lesbians and gays themselves to be heard. These allies make a difference. They reframe the status quo and encourage all of us to consider active change. (p. 81)

Whiteness: A Modern Invention

Historians have established that the category "white" was invented as recent as the seventeenth century in the Chesapeake Bay Colony to deal with tobacco and cotton plantation labor needs. Prior to that time there were many diverse ethnic categories but no "blacks" or "whites" (Allen 1997; Fine et al. 2002; Delgado & Stefrancic 1997).

In the seventeenth and eighteenth centuries people escaping oppressive conditions in Europe were frequently granted indentured servitude labor contracts that exchanged their ship passage to America for work and shelter for a specified number of years. As commerce and agriculture in the American colonies grew European shipping merchants addressed the growing labor shortage by engaging in bonded slave trade with costal tribes in West Africa. Early labels were "indentured" and "bonded", then "free" and "slave", then "Christian" and "non-Christian"—but there were Europeans who were non-Christian and Africans who were Christian so the labels "white" and "black" were invented by lawmakers of the Chesapeake Bay Colony to categorize heterogeneous groups in order to address the labor supervision problem.

Summary

The "we" and "they" of difference has allowed racism, discrimination, hatred, domination, and privilege of all kinds to exist on social and institutional levels since the beginning of human time. The personal relationships that form in counseling, psychotherapy, and education can promote a process of ongoing dialogue that can work to bridge worlds of difference.

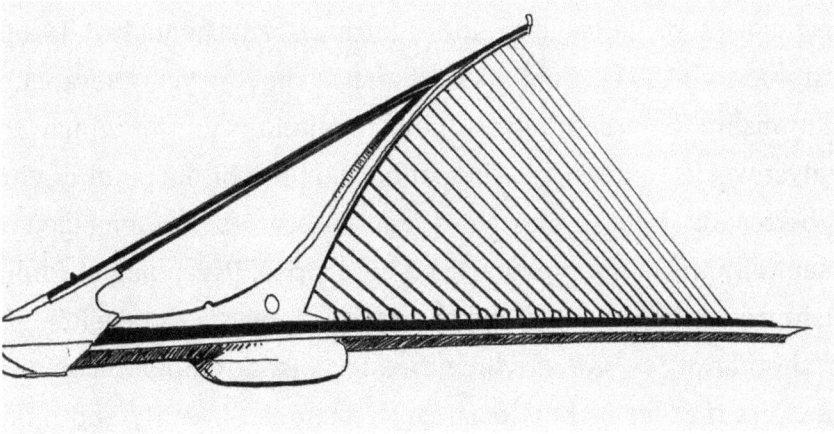

Perspective 8:
Cross-Cultural Diagnosis and Therapy

Postmodern constructionists, regardless of their theoretical orientations, are now clear that we all necessarily exist within socially and personally constructed realities whose implicit power intent is to keep us oriented and in control of the world as we have come to live it. The French philosopher Michel Foucault (1985, 1994) has made us aware that all theories—economic, social, educational, psychological or whatever—are essentially political acts. By political he means intentional activities in quest of power. According to Foucault, that all theories are implicitly ploys for power does not make them inherently bad, but dangerous—if we are not aware of how they take us in. Most dangerous are those theories that purport simply to describe objective reality while denying completely their biases and implicit intent to control and dominate.

Psychoanalyst Rudolf Ekstein (1984) asserts that theories of therapy are not so much ideas about how therapy works but statements of what therapists intend to do. The same can be said for theories of counseling and education. Psychoanalyst Joseph Natterson (1991) maintains that the psychotherapeutic relationship is essentially a power relationship in which the analyst works to persuade the patient that her or his point of view is better or right. Counselors and educators are engaged in essentially the same power-based enterprise. Psychologist Phillip Cushman (1995) highlights the power dimension of psychotherapy as one in which the therapist attempts to convince the client that his or her social constructions of reality and moral perspectives on life are more effective, more flexible, and generally better than those of the client—certainly positions also taken by counselors and educators.

Postmodern constructionism thus holds that counseling, psychotherapy, and education are all essentially political and moral expressions of our enmeshments in a series of cultural beliefs and practices that express our society's commitment to individualism and to a consumer economy. Counseling, psychotherapy, and educational practices are thus seen as intentional social, political, and moral acts arising out of our cultural, sociopolitical, and economic power structures in which sexism, classism, ageism, heterosexism, racism, consumerism, and individualism all play vital parts. However, Cushman (1995) has also shown that built into the theory and practice of many psychotherapies, notably relational psychotherapy and psychoanalysis, is the moral imperative that the power relations being lived in the moment between client and therapist in the transference and countertransference also be deconstructed (or analyzed). That is, simply trying to level the playing field is not enough. An explicit effort must be made to analyze at all moments in the interaction the power dimensions in play. Other psychotherapists as well as counseling and educational practitioners would do well to work towards building in to their work opportunities for joint studies of the power dimensions implicit in their own professional engagements.

Cross-Cultural Diagnosis

From the current Diagnostic and Statistical Manual of the American Psychiatric Association—the "DSM-IV":

> Clinicians are called upon to evaluate individuals from numerous different ethnic groups and cultural backgrounds (including many who are recent immigrants). Diagnostic assessment can be especially challenging when a clinician from one ethnic or cultural group uses the DSM-IV Classification to evaluate an individual from a different ethnic or cultural group. A clinician who is unfamiliar with the nuances of an individual's cultural frame of reference may incorrectly judge as psychopathology those normal variations in behavior, belief, or experience that are particular to the individual's culture. (American Psychiatric Association 1994, DSM-IV, p. xxiv)

The DSM-IV Outline for Cultural Formulations

Cultural identity of the individual (i.e., ethnic or cultural reference groups; degree of involvement in culture of origin and host culture; and language or languages used and preferred)

Cultural explanations of the individual's illness (e.g., nerves, somatic complaints, possessing spirits)

Cultural factors related to psychosocial environment and levels of functioning (e.g., stress in the local social environment; support provided by religion and kin networks)

Cultural elements of the relationship between the individual and the clinician (e.g., differences in culture and social status; difficulties emerging due to language problems; problems in negotiating a working relationship)

Overall cultural assessment for diagnosis and care (i.e., all cultural considerations that influence comprehensive diagnosis and care)" (DSM, pp. 40-41).

Interethnic Treatment Complications

Interethnic transference reactions often include overcompliance and friendliness; denial of ethnicity and culture; and mistrust, suspicion, and hostility. Many minority clients view "their own" as less competent than white middle-class professionals. Some minority therapists are often hardest on those like them for their dysfunctional lifestyles, or feel guilty about being more privileged. Interethnic countertransference can also result in over-identification, anger, cultural myopia, or distancing. Interethnic countertransference can arouse denial of ethnic/cultural differences, guilt, pity, aggression, and ambivalence (cited in Mishne, p. 184). The perspective of intersubjectivity to be discussed shortly is particularly well suited to cross-cultural therapy, because of the emphasis on verbal and nonverbal "meeting of minds," to use Aron's (1996) term.

Cross-Cultural Countertransference

"Today, Arab Israeli patients are increasingly appearing at outpatient clinics [in Israel], especially in areas with large Arab populations. They are also appearing at the university-based psychological services and they are beginning to turn to private psychotherapy" (Gorkin 1996, p. 159). For example:

> P., an unmarried Arab woman with masochistic features, informed her therapist that she had just discovered she was pregnant. She knew that she must have an abortion and was thinking of asking her sister and a friend from her village about where she might go for the procedure. The therapist, a Jewish male, encouraged P. to go right ahead and consult with her sister and friend. He completely overlooked the fact that his patient might be in danger if her parents, particularly her father, were to discover her mishap, which in their village would be regarded as an unpardonable disgrace for the family. The therapist failed to recognize that a course of action that would be sensible in his culture was for his patient probably a hazardous expression of her masochism. This oversight did not issue from any countertransferential sadism. It was simply, though dangerously, an initial failure to grasp the cultural meaning of the patient's intended action. Fortunately, the therapist was able to undo his error in time and to follow up with a useful exploration of the patient's masochism. (ibid.)

Four Common Countertransference Reactions

"In treating a patient from a very different background, the therapist is prone to countertransferential errors that reflect his cultural assumptions and values. He is also likely to err at times in understanding or construing the meaning of some of the patient's statements and behavior" (Gorkin 1996, p 169). Common errors are:

1. **Excessive Curiosity about the Patient's Culture**

   "One of the typical areas of countertransference difficulty is the therapist's pervasive, and occasionally hovering, curiosity about the patients cultural background.... cCultural material is explored more for its intrinsic interest than for its immediate relevance to the patient." (Gorkin 1996, p. 161)

2. **Making the Treatment Situation an Island**

   "[I]t is understandable that at times both therapist and patient may attempt to avoid discussion of their cultural differences. What happens...is that each of the participants cues the other that matters of cultural difference are extraneous or, in any event, beyond the pale of exploration." (ibid., p. 162)

3. **Countertransference Guilt**

   "Consciously or (more often) unconsciously, guilt reactions [in cross-cultural treatment situations enter] ... at some time or another.... Not uncommonly, the patient will evoke the therapist's guilt, in part as a means of camouflaging his personal difficulties." (ibid., p. 163).

4. **Aggression in the Countertransference**

   "Guilt and aggression are often intertwined and foster each other in countertransference reactions. For example when a Jewish therapist finds himself experiencing, in spite of his egalitarian ideology, persistent feelings of superiority toward the Arab patient. The therapist wants to regard the patient as an equal, and yet consciously or unconsciously he feels that the patient is from an 'inferior' culture." (ibid. p. 167)

In recent years there has been considerable discussion regarding so-called "countertransference disclosure." The field of psychotherapy inherited from Freud the "blank screen" model that effectively foreclosed any personal emotional involvement or disclosure on the part of the therapist. Recent analysis shows that what was foreclosed was in fact the therapist acknowledging or perhaps even knowing about his or her necessarily participatory role in the process. The point has been repeatedly made that in fact therapists are emotional participants and their clients know a great deal about them that can be effectively made use of as therapeutic grist for the mill. The question remains what kinds of disclosure are therapeutically appropriate under what circumstances (Hedges 1996, Aron 1996).

Indigenous Healing

Indigenous models of healing exist throughout the world. "For example, in many parts of West Africa, healing specialists known variously as herbalists, fetish men, mediums, healers, or sorcerers, employ spiritual forces to help address a variety of physical and emotional issues.

> In many Islamic countries, pins and fakirs are religious leaders within the Muslim faith who use verses from the Koran to treat illness. Sufis are secular traditional healers in these same regions who use music to treat psychological distress. In Mexico, curanderas (female) or curanderos (male), traditional healers, use herbalism and massage to alleviate mental and physical suffering. (Lee 1996, p. 87, cited in Sue et al.1996)

When considered from a Eurocentric psychoeducational perspective, these sources of help are often seen as primitive, unsophisticated, superstitious, unscientific, and potentially harmful to people in need of help. Says Lee (1996),

> In reviewing these non-Western indigenous helping methods, I have found some basic principles that

seem to form the foundation of the credibility and effectiveness of the healers who practice them. One can summarize these principles within the context of the Universal Shamanic Tradition (UST)....

First, most of these helping traditions are deeply rooted in religion and spiritualism. Unlike Western counseling and psychotherapy, which draw their focus from rationality and the scientific method, indigenous helping methods generally draw their emphasis from cosmological perspectives imbedded in cultural worldviews....

Second, in many indigenous helping systems, healers believe in many levels of human experience, which often include a spirit world where it is believed that answers to human destiny can be discerned. In many cultures, healers will 'journey' to these other levels of reality on behalf of people to find answers to their problems (Harner 1990). Some cultures induce this journey with drugs, while others use a monotonous percussion sound.

Third, most indigenous systems of healing take a holistic approach to helping, making little distinction between physical and mental well-being. Many indigenous healers perceive human distress as an indication that people have fallen out of harmony with both their internal and external environments.... (pp. 89-90)

Integrating Indigenous Models

Hickson and Mokhobo (1992) offer three options for integrating indigenous models of helping with counseling and therapy. First, they suggest introducing indigenous helpers into existing therapeutic interventions. Because of these helpers' influence among large sectors of certain communities, they could help individuals wary of or unfamiliar with Western counseling services. For example, "Concerning interventions with Cambodian refugee clients, Chan (1987) reports a mental-health agency that has a Buddhist monk on the counseling staff, which validates the Cambodian belief system and gives credibility to the counselors because they acknowledge the monk's healing powers" (p. 94).

As a second option for integrating indigenous healing, Hickson and Mokhobo offer a model of cooperation and collaboration. Though the counselor and the indigenous helper work independently of each other, they refer clients to each other when appropriate. For example, "Richardson (1991) ... suggests ways that counseling professionals can form collaborative relationships with ministers in the African-American church for the benefit of Black clients" (ibid.).

A third option Hickson and Mokhobo present is the combination of counseling with indigenous helping models to create a new therapeutic system. "Such systems have arisen in both rural and urban areas of the Midwest and Pacific northwest among health professionals in their efforts to treat substance abuse among Native-Americans. In many cases, counselors and related health professionals incorporate traditional Native-American healing practices, such as ceremonies, rituals, and prayers, into their substance-abuse treatment interventions. A traditional practice such as the "sweat lodge" adds a cultural and spiritual dimension to Eurocentric medical and psychological treatment initiatives. It also gives credence to the Native-American cultural value that the old ways are the best, because they have been proved (Richardson, 1981)" (ibid., p. 95).

Summary

While all theories of diagnosis and therapy are assumed to be essentially culturally biased and power-based, cross-cultural counseling, therapeutic and educational encounters seek to bridge worlds of difference by creating opportunities for dialogue and representation. Common to all healing traditions is the establishment of a relationship followed by a set of interactions aimed at relieving suffering through co-created representations. The universals involved in healing traditions appear to be:

1. The biologically driven attachment need,

2. The socially driven intersubjective exchange, and

3. The neurologically driven affective present moment.

Healers from many traditions have devised ways of tapping into these inherited and learned human characteristics in order to promote beneficial change. Widespread practices of modern-day counselors, psychotherapists, and educators wittingly and unwittingly tap into these centuries-old traditions for personal growth and healing. An illuminating analysis from anthropologist Claude Levi-Strauss of the psychodynamic mechanisms involved shamarita cures appears in Part III of this book.

Perspective 9: Intersubjectivity and Thirdness

I am a subject, an agent of my desires, thoughts, and actions. You are a subject, an agent of your desires, thoughts, and actions. When we come together for an intersubjective engagement over a period of time, something else begins to happen that affects us both. Intersubjective theories provide different ways of thinking about our intersubjective experiences.

According to this perspective psychotherapy (as well as counseling and education) are "pictured ... as a science of the intersubjective, focused on the interplay between the differently-organized subjective worlds of the observer and the observed" (Atwood & Stolorow 1984, p. 41).

The central theoretical construct of intersubjectivity theory is the "intersubjective field" defined as "a system composed of differently-organized, interacting subjective worlds" (Stolorow et al. 1987, p. ix). Stolorow and his colleagues use intersubjective "to refer to any psychological field formed by interacting worlds of experience, at whatever developmental level these worlds may be organized" (Stolorow & Atwood 1992, p. 3). The intersubjective field is often referred to as the intersubjective Third, the transference-countertransference matrix, or simply "the third person" in relationships.

"The concept of an intersubjective system brings to focus both the individual's world of [personal] experience and its embeddedness with other such worlds in a continual flow of reciprocal mutual influence" (ibid., p. 18). The subjectivity of individuals interacting in an intersubjective field is thus a critical aspect of cross-cultural encounters.

The goal of psychotherapy (as well as counseling and education) in the intersubjective view is for both participants in the context of a mutually-evolving, co-constructed intersubjectivity to come to recognize each other and to know themselves more fully in order to attain more flexibility, creativity, and passion in living and loving. The intersubjective perspective has enabled us to move our ideas about sexuality, culture, and ethnicity beyond the essentialist or naturalist individualistic drive conceptualizations that have been elaborated in the traditional intrapsychic perspective where the "myth of the isolated mind" has prevailed.

Intersubjectively considered, various sexual, cultural, and ethnicity interests, curiosities, and identity orientations become elaborated in relation to significant others early in life and then later manifest in different interpersonal and intersubjective contexts.

"[Intersubjective] recognition means that the other is mentally placed in the position of a different, outside entity but shares a similar feeling or state of mind. Separate minds and bodies can attune. When both individuals experience themselves as being transformed by the other, or by what they create in conjunction with the other, a choreography emerges that is not reducible to the idea of reacting to the outside" (Benjamin 1995, p. 202).

Summary

In recent years psychotherapy has undergone a radical change. The manifold ways in which we now try to grasp the meaning of the unconscious in terms of communication between ourselves and the other subject in the relationship have opened up the dialogic possibilities of intersubjectivity—nowhere more important than in cross-cultural encounters. While relational psychotherapists and psychoanalysts may be more explicit and determined in their efforts to study the intersubjective dimension, other kinds of therapists, counselors, and educators can equally well benefit from a study of how intersubjectivity operates in their field of endeavor.

Perspective 10: The Relational

A large international, multi-disciplinary group of theorists and therapeutic practitioners led by Stephen Mitchell and Louis Aron from New York University have collaborated to develop a "relational" perspective in which "the relationship" becomes a "third force" or "third participant" in therapy.

Heavily influenced by the feminist accent on eliminating the historically destructive male-subject/female-object dominance/submission split, the relational theorists emphasize that the human mind is not monadic but dyadic in nature—that human realities are mutually co-constructed. Vitalizing dynamic human relationships are seen as constituted by co-constructed intersubjective erotics—that is, by interpersonal interactions, dances, or idioms that are formulated as a "third" force or vector mutually created by and influencing both participants.

Features of Relational Psychotherapy

1. Symmetry exists between the two separate and equal subjectivities who engage each other toward achieving mutual recognition (and negation) in the intersubjective field of psychotherapy and psychoanalysis. Yet, asymmetry also characterizes the therapeutic situation, in that the therapist can be seen as an experienced expert, facilitator, and leader—although at times the asymmetrical roles can also reverse.

2. A co-creation of mutually achieved rhythms and harmonies of relating and the emergence of a co-constructed set of relational realities evolves in the therapeutic relationship that is rich, complex, and often confusing and contradictory. Mutually engaged ego and self boundaries are in constant flux between fruitful and dangerous interpenetrations.

3. The emergent sense of the importance and reality of the relationship itself (of "the analytic thirds") can be fruitfully studied by the therapeutic dyad.

4. Numerous dialectics of personality formation—for example, oedipal vs. preoedipal features, narcissistic investments vs. object love, depressive vs. manic affective splits, passive vs. active participation, and masculine vs. feminine gender attributes—all can be mutually experienced and worked through in a relational context.

5. A full array of developmentally-determined relational patterns can becomes mutually engaged and worked through in the transference/countertransference relational matrix.

6. Internalized personality functions and structures leading to increased personal flexibility, expanded interpersonal horizons, and novel possibilities for relating are thought to emerge from the relationally-centered treatment process. [source: Hedges 2003]

The Listening Perspectives Approach

The Listening Perspectives approach for therapists (Hedges 1983, 2003, 2005) aids in framing different qualities of internalized interpersonal relatedness experience as they arise in the here-and-now therapeutic relationship. Both the Listening Perspectives approach and Relational Psychotherapy abandon entirely the naïve view that we can ever objectively consider how things really are or that the human mind can ever be studied in isolation from the intersubjective fields in which human beings live. My original 1983 text provides an overview of the development of a century of psychoanalytic concepts and practices. I organized the ideas along an axis of self and other relatedness possibilities from the earliest and simplest relational forms to the more complex triangular and symbolic forms. The Listening Perspectives approach to therapy maintains that all we can ever do with any degree of certainly is to generate perspectives, perceptual angles, or empathic stances from which to listen in order to frame what people have to tell us and to the ways in which two people engage each other in the therapeutic relationship.

The Listening Perspectives way of approaching the psychotherapeutic situation encourages us as professional listeners to experience ourselves as living human participants involved in a full emotional relationship with someone endeavoring to experience and to express his or her life experience.

The Listening Perspectives approach further encourages us to formulate our work in terms of theories that enhance the listening and speaking possibilities within a living, breathing, here-and-now relationship rather than with theories that seek to reify or personify psychological concepts or to capture the "true nature" of the human mind as objectively defined.

I have formulated four distinctly different ways of listening—ways of being with people in psychotherapy. These four Listening Perspectives use metaphors borrowed from human development to describe four kinds of human relatedness potentials. These four kinds of relational possibilities are assumed to be universal but are experienced and valued differently in different cultural settings.

I. THE ORGANIZING EXPERIENCE: Infants require certain forms of connection and interconnection in order to remain psychologically alert and enlivened to themselves and to others. In their early relatedness they are busy "organizing" physical and mental channels of connection—first to mother's body, later to her mind and to the minds of others—for nurturance, stimulation, soothing, and evacuation. Framing organizing patterns for analysis entails studying how two people approach to make connections and then turn away, veer off, rupture, or dissipate the intensity of the connections.

II. THE SYMBIOTIC EXPERIENCE: Toddlers are busy learning how to make emotional relationships (both good and bad) work for them. They experience a sense of merger and reciprocity with their primary caregivers, thus establishing many knee-jerk, automatic, characterological, and role-reversible patterns or scenarios of relatedness. Framing the symbiotic relatedness structures for analysis entails noting how each person characteristically engages the other and how interactive scenarios evolve from two subjectively-formed sets of internalized self-and-other interaction patterns.

III. THE SELF-OTHER EXPERIENCE: Two- and three-year-olds are preoccupied with using the acceptance and approval of others for developing and enhancing self-definitions, self-skills, and self-esteem. Their relatedness strivings use the mirroring, twinning, and idealizing responses of significant others to firm up their budding sense of self. Framing for analysis the self-other patterns used for affirming, confirming, and inspiring the self entails studying how the internalized mirroring, twinning, and idealizing patterns used in self-development in the pasts of both participants play out to enhance and limit the possibilities for mutual self-to-self-other resonance in the emerging interpersonal engagement.

IV. THE INDEPENDENCE EXPERIENCE: Four- to seven-year-olds are dealing with triangular love and hate relationships and are moving toward more complex social relationships. In their relatedness they experience others as separate centers of initiative and themselves as independent agents in a socially-competitive environment. Framing the internalized patterns of independently-interacting selves in both cooperative and competitive triangulations with real and fantasized third parties entails studying the emerging interaction patterns for evidence of repressive forces operating within each participant and between the analytic couple that work to limit or spoil the full interactive potential. (Hedges, 2003, 2005)

Summary of the Listening Perspectives Approach

Internalized relatedness patterns from the lived past of each participant as well as novel configurations emerging from the interpersonal engagement of therapy are an expectable focus of discussion as the therapeutic relationship unfolds (Hedges 2005). Emotional honesty about and limited disclosure of affective experience on the part of the analyst will be an expectable part of the emerging therapeutic relationship (Maroda 1999). The development of a personal creative style of relating that integrates, like postmodern art, a variety of ideas and interventions into the specific therapeutic exchange will be another expectable aspect of the emergent dialogue (Johnson 1991). A multiplicity of ways of viewing and working together with the internalized patterns of both people, and the emerging configurations of interaction characteristic of the couple, can also be expected (Stark 1994, 1997).

The four relatedness Listening Perspectives are based on developmental *metaphors* of how a growing child potentially engages and is engaged by others in interpersonal interactions that build internal habits, structures, or patterns of relational expectation during different age periods. Differential framing secures for psychotherapeutic study the *structures, patterns, configurations*, and/or *modes* of internalized interpersonal interaction that have characterized the past interactions of both participants and that are transferred into and resisted conscious awareness and expression in the current mutually developing therapeutic relationship. In counseling settings and in some educational settings it is useful to be able to define what level of relatedness possibilities are being activated or lived by two people in a relational moment. These perspectives guide such definitions.

Relatedness Listening Perspectives thus formed do *not* represent a developmental schema, but rather serve to identify a general array of relatedness possibilities lived out each day in various ways by all people.

Relational psychotherapists rightly or wrongly have been repeatedly criticized on the basis that there is little *systematic* attention to transference, resistance, and countertransference in relational work. In contrast, the relatedness Listening Perspectives have been explicitly defined for the purposes of bringing out the unconscious transference/resistance and countertransference/counter-resistance relatedness dimensions perennially at play in the therapeutic relationship.

The relatedness Listening Perspectives approach considers psychotherapeutic concepts valuable and viable only insofar as they are formulated specifically within a human listening (relational) context. Psychotherapeutic knowledge cannot be about a thing, the human mind, but rather exists as *a body of thought about how people are able to achieve mutually enlivening consciousness-raising experiences in an emotionally alive and emotionally stressful relationship* (Friedman 1988).

Conclusions

The evolving dynamics or erotics of the mutually co-constructed therapeutic relationship allow for the opening of new space and new tensions in which the dance of Thirdness can appear and be jointly negotiated toward mutual regulations and transformations. We can no longer simply take anyone's stated cultural, ethnic, or sexual orientations or gender identities at face value in life or in counseling, psychotherapy, or education. Through cross-cultural encounters we seek to bridge worlds of difference while remaining ever mindful of the biases both participants bring to the relationship.

Part II:
Cross-Cultural Encounters from the Psychotherapy Literature

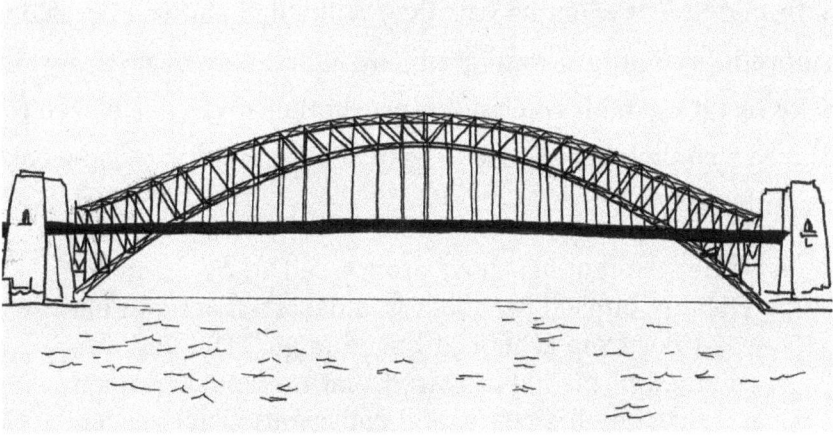

The perspectives outlined in Part I provide various ways of considering cross-cultural encounters in counseling, psychotherapy, education, and life in general. We now move to consider a series of such encounters reported in the psychotherapy literature that afford an opportunity to see, as it were, in slow motion what some of the factors are that may be operating in different intercultural situations.

Willie: "I want those people and that place back" —RoseMarie Pérez Foster[3]

Willie's story reminds us of how firmly we tend to cling to our own suppositions about people and their unconscious expressions. Born in the Dominican Republic and emigrating with his family to the United States when he was five, Willie had showed occasional encopretic symptoms that gradually worsened over the years, finally resulting in his referral for psychotherapy at age eleven to a children's clinic where Foster began seeing him for twice-weekly psychotherapy.

> Willie's soiling had now progressed to occasionally relieving himself outdoors in a deserted area on his way to or from school "if I need to go." The boy was ashamed of his habit, feared that he would be seen as "dirty" by his peers, and conscientiously washed himself and changed clothes after soiling himself. (p. 10)

Upon psychiatric examination he was diagnosed with "secondary encopresis of functional etiology," his soiling being seen as having a psychological rather than biological basis. After soiling himself he washed meticulously which seen as a defense against rageful outbursts. His play showed militaristic themes, which were seen as obsessive-compulsive attempts to contain his anal-sadistic urges. His quiet demeanor was interpreted as emotional constriction caused by the fear of dangerous explosive rage. In short, his symptomatology was

---

[3] Foster, R. P. "What is a Multicultural Perspective for Psychoanalysis?" In R. P. Foster et al. (Eds.). (1996). *Reaching Across Boundaries of Culture and Class: Widening the Scope of Psychotherapy.* Lanham, MD: Rowman & Littlefield Publishers.

formulated as stemming from an obsessive-compulsive personality with anal-sadistic preoccupations accompanied by defensive rituals that precariously controlled outbursts of rage, resulting in limitations in his overall expressive functioning. Foster describes her therapy sessions:

> Willie was a handsome, sturdily built boy whose gentle and smiling social manner only momentarily covered a sad and preoccupied face when at rest. He was quite tense and had difficulty speaking freely with me, such that we almost entirely interacted through symbolic play. His fantasies described lost people, houses, and animals swept away by destructive forces, and soldiers parading in uniform. (p. 10)

After six months of therapy Willie's mother disclosed that he was not her biological child, but had been adopted shortly before leaving the Dominican Republic from a poor family with twelve children who had gladly relinquished him with the hope that life in the United States would afford him significantly improved opportunities. Foster herself was familiar with La Romana province where Willie came from and explains that such adoptions are not unusual in the international culture of poverty. She describes La Romana as a beautifully lush but sadly impoverished countryside. The people are mostly sharecroppers making a sustenance living without benefit of electricity or agricultural technology. There are certainly no indoor toilets and toddlers amble about unclothed in the heat, often relieving themselves wherever it is convenient. Young people only speak when spoken to by adults (appearing here as emotional constriction) but family life is rich and full of love. Writes Foster:

Willie's case frustrates and shames me when I think of the misplaced emphasis of my early theoretical formulations. While busy searching for the anal-aggressive data that would substantiate my psychodynamic formulation (and intellectual narcissism!), I had missed the painful elements of Willie's reality. Adopted by caring people who had unquestionably improved his physical standard of living, Willie had nevertheless been terminally separated from his mother and the world that he knew. As I would later hear from him, Willie's letting go, especially during times of stress, was his way of returning to Mother and his early life, which for him had included the option to relieve himself outdoors at will. Abandonment, feeling like a lost child in a strange world, and the sense that everything he knew around him could disappear suddenly, were the inner psychic reality in which Willie lived. (p. 11)

His therapist painfully confesses that she believes Willie had tried to communicate his plight to her in many of his play sessions but that her search for data that would confirm her preconceived diagnostic formulations had made her deaf to what Willie had to say to her. He undoubtedly experienced much reactive anger, but the trauma leading to the increase of his stress symptoms was not derived from supposed controls around anal concerns but rather from the imposed separation from the life he had known and the people whom he had loved. Although there may have been elements of auto-erotic stimulation in his defecation practices, as held by the classical view, Willie himself was finally able to tell her that defecating freely when he felt like it was part of an attempt to retrieve the safety and love from his early world. "I used to live in a place," he said, "where people let me do this. I want those people and that place back" (p. 11).

Manash: "Community Dedication"
—RoseMarie Pérez Foster[4]

Foster relates another cross-cultural encounter that was difficult for her to understand and even more difficult for her to offer help of any kind for. Twenty-nine-year-old Manash suffered from severe depression as a political refugee from a middle-eastern country that had been militarily occupied by an oppressive foreign power. He spoke fluent English as a second language and was able to explain to her that all of the meaning of his life had completely vanished as a result of his exile.

Manash had been born into a semi-religious cast where the men of his family traditionally assumed an obligation for community service and social group welfare. Having been groomed his entire life to fulfill his family vocation, the political take-over had now deprived him of all sense of belongingness, self-fulfillment, and purpose—his entire life destiny had been totally obliterated. Manash was living in painful exile entirely bereft of meaning.

> I struggled to understand Manash's inner sense of loss for many months, while also noting that he was a resourceful man who had managed to start a small import business that was affording him an [adequate] income. I also struggled with personal and theoretical assumptions about what makes people feel stable and whole. Manash appeared resilient and creative. Surely he would soon find other ways of repairing his sense of narcissistic injury. But he didn't. (p. 13)

---

[4] Ibid.

Foster struggles with values and assumptions that fill her mind as a Western trained clinician—values of individualism and self-fulfillment based on individual successes and pride in autonomous achievement. Manash, on the other hand, sought his sense of uniqueness and worth in fulfilling his assigned role in the life of the group. She points out that Americans struggle to be free of family influences and group constraints in order to fulfill their individually chosen destinies and that Western trained therapists are immersed in values of individuation, autonomy, personal separateness, and pride based on individual achievement. Manash's sense of what it meant to be well-developed and whole proved to be a world away from hers as she reports being at a total loss of how to help him recover his sense of self-esteem and purpose under the drastically changed political and cultural conditions.

A Japanese Therapist: "We are working together" —Alan Roland[5]

Roland relates a cross-cultural incident from a psychoanalytic training case conference situation that illustrate how our Western assumptions about self can lead us to sadly misunderstand people from other cultural orientations. The story was told to him some years later by Japanese psychoanalyst who had trained in this country and later returned to Japan to practice.

In the case conference the analyst had presented an initial hour with a twenty-year-old Japanese woman who was somewhat hesitant to tell him about the problems she was having with her American boyfriend. He had listened attentively and said very

---

[5] Roland, A. "How Universal is the Psychoanalytic Self?" In Foster et al., ibid.

little during the hour. At the close of the session he said, "Now that we are working together, we shall continue in future sessions" (p. 71). The senior analyst leading the case conference was astonished at the way he ended the session and asked, "How come you said 'now that we are working together' when there was very little if any verbal exchange or interaction between the two of you?" Her question frustrated the analyst-in-training because he felt that she was not understanding him as a Japanese and that she seemed unable to grasp the appropriateness of his comment to his Japanese patient.

Asks Roland, "what very different assumptions about selves and relationships were the American trainer and the Japanese student working with?" Roland points out that the instructor, as most of us would, assumed that in therapy there are two individuals speaking together with one free-associating and the other clarifying or interpreting. The Western individualistically experienced I-selves, each with discernable ego boundaries, produces the sense of an "I" and "you" engagement that leads to an exchange of expertise for a fee—even though American egalitarianism sees both as participants free and equal agents.

On the other hand, Roland tells us, the Japanese therapist assumes different kinds of selves and very different kinds of communication to be present in a therapeutic interaction. This therapist is working from the "we-self" of the Japanese—a self that is primarily experienced in relation to others and is integral to Japanese-style hierarchical relationships in which subordinate and superior "form a 'we' relationship that is quite different from American egalitarianism" (p. 72). For the Japanese a sense of individual I-ness in wanting or wishing in the Western sense seldom exists. Instead, Japanese depend on each other to sense what they want.

> The therapist knew from Japanese-style hierarchical relationships, and from years of psychotherapy experience in Japan, that in order for any therapy to take place he had to foster the development of a close "we" relationship between superior-therapist and subordinate-patient. In Japan, unlike for the most part in America, the superior is expected to be empathically nurturing and responsible to the subordinate. He further knew that in their society that so stresses the correct presentation of self (*omote*) in a rigorously observed social etiquette, particularly in the formal hierarchical relationships, Japanese keep a highly private, secretive self (*ura*) in which all kinds of feelings, fantasies, and thoughts are present (Doi 1986, Roland 1988). This is a self that is to be empathically sensed and not intruded upon. Only after considerable time, when a trusting relationship has been formed and the therapy relationship has been gradually transformed from an outsider one (*solo*) to an insider one (*uchi*) will a Japanese begin to share important aspects of his or her inner life. Thus, this Japanese therapist was silently empathic with his patient, a not unusual way of communicating in Japan, where both patient and therapist, as in other hierarchical relationships, expect the other to empathically sense what each is feeling and thinking, often with a minimum of overt communication (Roland 1988). There is, after all, a saying in Japan, "Nothing important is ever to be communicated verbally." (p. 72)

In Roland's extensive studies of psychotherapy as practiced in Japan and India he continually reminds us of how many ways our Western sense of self and relationships differ from those in the East (Roland 1988).

Rosa: "Missed Appointments" —Neil Altman[6]

Another set of cross-cultural issues arises in the assumptions about *how* therapeutic relationships are to be conducted—assumptions that permeate the entire culture of psychotherapy. We expect our clients to arrive with presenting complaints they can articulate; to understand that if we are to help them they must come to sessions regularly to achieve continuity; to see how relationship problems on the outside tend to re-emerge in the therapy setting; to be respectful of our personal and professional boundaries around such issues as showing up on time, properly cancelling missed appointments, and timely payment for services; and to honor our established practices in taking breaks from therapy and in terminating the therapeutic relationship. Our psychotherapy training attaches culture-bound meanings to all of these relationship issues—meanings and practices which it is often difficult for us to relinquish or transcend in the countertransference of cross-cultural professional work.

Altman speaks to us about his relationship with Rosa, a high school senior who has recently broken up with a boyfriend and is now experiencing severe panic attacks and intermittent depression. Rosa is the oldest of five children from parents who emigrated here twenty years ago from the Dominican Republic. Rosa's mother was a bright woman who chose to remain at home to raise the children and had never learned English. Rosa's father was a bright and ambitious man who had worked his way up from a stock clerk to a general manager of a store and who was doing quite well.

---

[6] Altman, N. (1995). *The Analyst in the Inner City*. The Analytic Press: New Jersey, London.

After Rosa's boyfriend left her for another girl she fell into deep depression with suicidal thoughts and started twice weekly therapy with Altman. It might be added that Neil Altman's background is middle-class, Jewish, with advanced education in psychoanalysis and research as well as humanitarian interest that has led him to work part time in a community clinic in lower Manhattan where he could study the problems of attempting to apply and/or to modify traditionally conceived therapeutic processes to fit lower-socioeconomic class and cross-cultural contexts.

After a few sessions Rosa began missing sessions, at first calling to cancel with an excuse related to school activities or to helping her mother at home. Then came missed sessions without cancellations which left Altman sad and disappointed since he felt that the two of them were hitting it off pretty well. Rosa was an upwardly mobile young woman with much to gain from therapeutic involvement. In this regard she was like many of the clients Altman was seeing at the clinic—people with great potentials but hopelessly despairing and seemingly enmeshed in intractable life situations. The missed appointments caused Altman to feel betrayed in what he saw as their joint project in freeing Rosa up from childhood constraints and successfully launching her into a new and more promising life.

> After the pattern of keeping and missing appointments had established itself, I developed a characteristic conflict about how to follow up on the missed appointments. I felt caught between intruding by pursuing her and abandoning her by seeming to ignore her absence. I also felt caught between revealing to her, by an overly eager phone call, how much I wanted her to show up and

revealing to her, by withholding contact, how angry I was. My compromise solution was to wait a day or two to see if she would call; if she did not, I would write her a letter noting that she had missed an appointment and saying that unless I heard otherwise, I would expect to see her at our next appointment. Rosa would show up at the next appointment with some concrete reason she had been unable to come to the appointment and apologize for having forgotten to call me. (pp. 13-14)

When Rosa failed to respond to one of his notes he sent a follow-up note and she did call to set up an appointment. Upon inquiry, she explained that she had been feeling better and wasn't feeling a need to come regularly, but since he was the doctor she was not inclined to challenge his authority. When asked about how she felt he might experience her failure to cancel, she said she had wondered how he would fill his time and worried that he might be angry about having been "stood up." Altman quickly related this to her anger at having been "stood up" by her boyfriend, a formulation which she quickly accepted.

In the next session, Rosa expressed anger at her mother for insisting that she be home at midnight the previous weekend when she had gone to a party. She felt that her mother could not accept that she was pretty much grown up. What if she wanted to go away to college the next year? Would her mother even let her go? Rosa felt that her mother had no life of her own, that she would go into a depression if Rosa did not stay home with her. I suggested that Rosa might feel similarly about me, that she had to hide her thought that she was feeling better and might not need me anymore. Rosa agreed and said that she had also been feeling angry at me for pursuing her when she thought she was making it

99

clear by her absence that she did not want to come to her sessions, at least on a regular basis. Her mother and I were both standing in the way of her developing autonomy. (p.14)

Over the next few sessions—which were not missed—Rosa explored her past guilt over leaving her friends to go uptown to a private school and her present guilt over wanting to leave her mother to go to college. On the one hand she experienced Altman like her mother as holding back her independent development while on the other hand she experienced him like her father as trying to remove obstacles to her moving away from mother and developing herself. Rosa was able to articulate her fear that her father harbored covert sexual feelings toward her—for example, at times he would speak to her in English to deliberately exclude her mother. But she was unable to acknowledge any sexual feelings that might be between her and her therapist.

Rosa continued therapy off and on during her senior year and did go away to college but soon dropped out in favor of a school closer to home. From time to time over the next few years she would call Altman when she was feeling particularly distressed and seemed to benefit from talking with him.

Altman concludes indicating how this case illustrates complications of work in impoverished and/or immigrant neighborhoods. Complicating factors include gender, ethnicity, culture, and socioeconomic status as they appear in transference and countertransference. With Rosa, far from simply thwarting therapeutic progress, Altman believes that the missed appointments and his response to them served as crucial catalysts in developing a productive therapeutic relationship. The problem lies, says Altman, in our attempting to project our own ideas about how therapy is to proceed onto people and circumstances that are so very different from our own cultural mindsets.

José: "Growing Up" —Neil Altman[7]

Similar cross-cultural difficulties arose in Altman's work with José, a sixteen-year-old high school junior who had been removed from his mother's custody a year earlier when he and his younger brother were found living in a park with their mother during one of her frequent psychotic breaks. He had developed a number of compulsive rituals and obsessive thoughts which lifted early in therapy, gradually giving way to frequent thoughts of impending doom. Altman learns that over the years when his mother would go into one of her psychotic states it was his responsibility to care for his younger brother since there had never been a father present. José would not go to school until he was sure everything was okay at home.

At the group home and in alternative school he endeared himself to his caregivers and teachers as a bright, hard-working, and promising boy. He later graduated valedictorian of his class and was awarded a scholarship to college.

> I saw José once a week for a year until he graduated. He spoke softly and undemonstratively, yawning a lot. I, too, found it hard to keep my eyelids from drooping when I was with him. As the year went on, José began having intrusive thoughts about hurting his mother. He was horrified. I tried to encourage him to tolerate these thoughts and to differentiate them from actions. One day, however, José came in and told me that he had thrown a rock through the window of his mother's new apartment. Now I was

---

[7] Ibid.

horrified, too, and I began to feel that I had been too quick to assume thoughts and actions could be differentiated for José. I also developed a new appreciation for his rage and how the somnolent atmosphere in the sessions may have been a cover for these feelings. I now had to find a way to approach José's angry feelings without complacently assuming that verbalization would ensure control or that we could handle what would emerge if we opened this Pandora's box.... [A]s we continued our work, rage receded as an issue as José's life became quite stable and satisfying; it seemed he had created a new family for himself with his group home counselors, his high school teachers, and me. (p. 16)

After high school, however, José quickly began dismantling his support system, leaving the group home before it was actually necessary, renting a room in the home of a former teacher, and dropping out of therapy. Altman speculates that he was handling his chronic fears of abandonment by leaving the home early, by ending therapy before Altman terminated him, and by holding onto high school by renting a room from his teacher. Altman attempted to prolong therapy during this turbulent period but José seemed determined to be in control of his own life.

Altman concludes this episode of early growth followed by an acting out of the repeated abandonments by his mother with:

I next heard from José about six months later. He had not entered college and planned to work for a year and save some money. He had started work as a stock boy in a store and had so impressed his superiors that he was promoted several times. He had also started to drink heavily. He called me after he missed work one day without calling in, the day after receiving a major promotion. In addition, he had begun stealing liquor from the former teacher

from whom he was renting his room. He thought he
was probably about to be caught and thrown out. He
saw that he was sabotaging his success and thought
it was time to come back to therapy. (p. 17)

We can hope that after this somewhat checkered therapy beginning that José's subsequent therapy helped him locate the numerous internal sources of self-sabotage. This episode illustrates how difficult it is even for the brightest of people to extricate themselves from internalized ghosts of the past.

Norma: "Skin Color Transference" —RoseMarie Pérez Foster[8]

Psychologist Pratyusha Tummala-Nara has researched the issues involved in skin color worldwide. She concludes that in most cultures throughout the world power and domination are associated with a light skin color. "Preference for light skin divides and shapes identity and experience within various ethnic communities; it has a significant impact on psychological adjustment and contributes to an increased understanding of the experiences of ethnic minorities; it perpetuates the myth of lower capacities for people of color and contributes to divisions within ethnic groups" (Tummala-Nara, cited in Morris 2005, p. 59).

As I researched for this book I was reminded again and again of how profoundly skin color affects people in diverse circumstances and how often it appears in the transference-countertransference matrix. Of course, skin color per se isn't the sole issue, but a host of other physical and psychological features that have become associated (rightly or wrongly) with skin color. What follows are

---

[8] Foster, ibid.

several clinical accounts in which skin color and its associated meanings have come into play.

Of Latin descent, psychotherapist Foster describes herself as light-skinned with blue eyes and curly hair. She reminds us of the rich racial mixing that characterizes Hispanic people—strands of Indian, European, and African genes mixed to give a wide variety of appearances, even within close-knit families.

Foster describes how, about a year into her psychodynamic psychotherapy work with Norma, a chemical engineer of Panamanian descent, she noted that the issues of race and skin color had never come up—despite the fact that Norma had specifically sought therapy with her because of her Latin background. Norma is described as a strikingly beautiful young woman with light cocoa skin, brown eyes, and very curly, shoulder-length hair.

One rainy day the patient commented that it looked as if her therapist had cut her hair. Foster explained how her hair becomes curlier in the humidity. This opened a discussion that had been long overdue and turned out to be most illuminating. It seems that Norma had been a close observer of Foster's hairstyle over the year and had concluded that she blow dries her hair to keep it from curling so much. Foster nervously inquires on.

> She had also surmised that I probably did not like my hair, because it is the thing that made me look the most Hispanic. Her exploration of the inner me continued: she described the physical characteristics of my parents and grandparents, the percent distribution of the various races in my blood by virtue of my features, the coloring of my husband and children, and how I felt about all of them.

> Inevitably this exploration finally turned to Norma's own family. She had been the darkest-skinned of all her siblings. Not only had she been mocked for this and accused of not being her fair-skinned father's child, but also, because of her color, she was offered no hope of succeeding in a white-dominated world. Norma had hidden her racial pain, assuming that I would also dislike her for being a dark-skinned girl. (p. 16)

Despite initial nervousness in the countertransference, the exploration led to a clarification of many issues including Norma's negative self-image, her racial pain, her agony over the distance her parents and family kept, and her beliefs about her limitations as a dark-skinned woman in a world dominated by light skin and male privilege.

Much later in treatment Norma was to refer back many times to this discussion in which she felt her therapist's "permission to get into your head." By being able to deal with racial issues in projected form first Norma was able to allow herself to experience her own feelings and pain and then to develop new avenues of self-esteem based on her racialized identification with her highly successful and well-esteemed therapist.

> Norma's [painfully accurate] perception of my own unspoken conflict, and her effort not to threaten my equilibrium would have truncated open exploration of her own sense of racial inferiority. In other words, she would have come to know my secrets, but at great expense to herself silently permitted me to hide them. (p. 17)

How often are we called upon as professionals with ever so many dynamic issues like skin color to sit still while clients and students work over their perceptions and projections about various painful parts of ourselves so that they can come to know themselves better? Issues around skin color, racial bias, and male dominance have affected us all in various ways in our identity structures and other personality features as well. Allowing honest exploration of these often sensitive issues is a vital aspect of counseling, psychotherapy, and education.

Juanita: "Skin Color Rejection" —Cheryl Thompson[9]

Earlier in the listening perspective of ghosts and transgenerational haunting we examined the intertwining nature of internal conflicts arising from one's own past experience, from one's position in the social order, and from inherited experiences of forbearers. Nowhere is the complexity of these three sources of internalization more evident that in professional work with African-Americans.

Thirty-one-year-old Juanita entered treatment complaining of isolation. As a teacher she attributed much of her isolation to hatred in her colleagues. But even with the three other African-American teachers at her school she felt excluded by schedules and prior commitments. She explained that she ate her lunch by herself in her classroom because she didn't feel welcome in the cafeteria, and that her attempts to participate in conversation were ignored.

Juanita's relation with her mother was characterized mostly by Mother delivering humiliating diatribes of criticism with the intent to hurt and reject. Her mother only accepted her when they were alone. When other family members were present she felt ignored.

---

[9] Cheryl L. Thompson, "The African-American Patient in Psychodynamic Treatment." In R.P. Foster et al. (Eds.), ibid.

As the oldest of three children, Juanita lived most of her childhood with her divorced mother, her grandmother, her aunt, and two siblings. She came from an essentially middle-class family where skin color was part of the attribution of middle-class status. Juanita initially experienced herself as favored by her aunt and her grandmother. However, she described herself as falling from grace once she began to make friends with the neighborhood children. The following two vignettes helped us disentangle and begin to understand the patient's morass of rejection and isolation.

At about age 7, Juanita was playing with a neighborhood child when her aunt came outside and sent the child away, yelling at the patient that she was not to play with that child because she was too dark-skinned. The patient needed to deny the perception that the child rejected by her caretakers was more like her mother in appearance than anyone else in the family.... When the patient became angry with her mother and devalued her, she raged at her for not protecting her from the aunt and grandmother. She was unable to see that her mother could not protect her because she too was a victim of the same rejection.

When she was 20, Juanita spent the summer in a theater company where she became friends with a young white man. She invited him to her home to meet her family. After the family visit, she stopped being friendly with him because she felt the young man did not accept her more obviously black mother. (p. 119)

The emergence of these memories helped Juanita to uncover the denial of her mother's pain and victimization. Further she began to realize how much her mother idealized her because of her light skin and believed she could gain the much-needed family acceptance through her daughter's light skin. Having gained empathy for her mother through therapy, she was able to open a discussion that led to the revelation that her unacceptable mother was not her grandmother's child but no doubt the offspring of some extended relative's indiscretion. It seems that the family had come to use skin color as a symbol of loose libidinous urges. Juanita's own interest in boys, theater, and dancing caused further rejection—because libidinal freedom makes African-Americans appear to be "lazy, childlike, negroes."

Juanita managed to avoid serious dating and intimate relating because white boys would draw too much attention and black boys were only interested in sex. As Juanita began to understand some of the internalized sources of her perceived rejections, she began to eat in the school cafeteria, to form friendships with colleagues, to join a black teachers group for the improvement of education, and to date. Juanita is a gifted teacher and, now that she feels less internal rejection, an important asset to her community.

In the transference of therapy she continued into the fourth year to idealize her therapist as the doctor who could do no wrong, though she slowly began to experience misunderstandings as rejection and at last to experience disappointments in the therapist as internalized rejections. Thompson feels that Juanita's treatment illustrates many of the issues involved in skin color, family relationships, and family secrets that are ubiquitous in professional work with African-Americans.

Charles: "A Fear of Black Women" —Cheryl Thompson[10]

Charles has always feared and disliked Black women. But he has feared getting into fights and getting hurt if he dates White women. He is especially afraid that his therapist will reject him because of his fear and dislike of Black women.

Charles had experienced both painful rejection and boundary-less seduction from his mother, leaving him with a schism between bad Black women and good White women. After he was able to assess that Thompson would not reject him because of his love-object choice he began in the sixth year of treatment to understand that his mother had been completely unable, not unwilling, to mother him. In understanding her inability to mother him he came also to understand the many hurtful things he had done to women—essentially as cruel role-reversal identifications.

In his work Charles was always underappreciated and underpaid. He could barely afford dormitory-style living and managed to get in frequent fights. As he began to understand his need to place himself in physical danger and to create enemies, he gradually worked toward building friendships and improving his work situation. As the curtain drops on Charles, he has more therapy to do, but for the first time in his life he has a stable well-paying job, a home of his own, enough to pay tuition for his Master's degree, and now some friends to share his life with. He has come to see his past as acting out his internalized sense of isolation, endangerment, and self-deprivation.

Charles defines therapeutic change as enabling him to move from a daily survival mode to creating ongoing opportunities for

---

[10] Ibid.

life. To me, Charles' therapy illustrates a movement from an early and faulty internalization of personal and racialized inferiority to the possibility of living without such culturally-burdened constraints. It also illustrates how the destructive color-tagging of culture can be pressed into service of personal love-object splitting left over from early childhood. That is, how Charles' fear and dislike of Black women has nothing to do with race per se, and everything to do with early experiences of good and bad mothering that distortedly come to assume racial significance.

"Black Patient/White Analyst" —Neil Altman[11]

Altman describes the opening sessions of therapy between a White middle class educated analyst and a 40-year-old African-American man of similar educational and class background. In response to the analyst's question of why he is choosing a White therapist, the patient indicates that he knows several Black therapists but feels they would be leading him into identification with minority and poverty issues that he has little interest in and urging him to hate Whites which he isn't interested in either.

In the countertransference Altman feels a sense of security in the alliance implicitly being made by them in disdaining those Blacks who seek simple solutions to complex problems by blaming Whites. He also feels relieved that this Black man doesn't hate him as White, won't direct suspicion and mistrust toward him, won't uncover his hidden racism.

> On the other hand, the analyst felt uneasy that this alliance was based on creating a common "enemy." The dynamic seemed too similar to what the patient

---

[11] Altman, N. "The Accommodation of Diversity in Psychoanalysis." In R. P. Foster et al. (Eds.), ibid.

was describing in terms of black people forging solidarity out of hatred of whites. Further, he wondered if he were not being asked to collude with the patient's defensive denial of his own anger, his own sense of being oppressed, his own multifaceted identification with black people and/or lower socioeconomic status people. Finally, the analyst wondered if he were not being asked to collude with a denial of his racism, as if the two of them could create a black-white partnership that would be devoid of mistrust and hostility. The patient seemed to be stimulating the analyst's racism while simultaneously inviting him to deny the existence of such feelings between the two of them. Class solidarity, perhaps, was being used to deny racial difference and potential discordance. (p. 199)

This brief description of the opening gambit of therapy suggests to me that even cross-cultural or interethnic situations that might at first appear to be therapeutically tenable or even optimal are necessarily loaded with complications crying out to be explored. What often differs in counseling, psychotherapy, and educational settings from other life settings is that we have the opportunity to put the issues on the table and to unpack whatever may be threateningly implicit in otherwise benign-looking packages.

Louise: "Resistances to Self-Definition" —Cheryl Thompson[12]

Fifty-year-old African-American social worker, Louise, was the first in her family to obtain a college degree. Louise entered treatment because she felt pained at experiencing herself as unattractive, un-feminine, and essentially unlovable. People

---

[12] C. Thompson, ibid.

around her saw her as attractive, strong, independent, and caring but she could not bring herself to express to her husband or to her family that she had her own emotional needs.

> Race immediately presented itself as a significant source of her conflict. Louise is an extremely light-skinned African-American woman. She has found herself having to defend her blackness in interaction with blacks as well as whites. Louise spent her childhood in a small southern town in which her family had much status as a result of her father's position, size, and biracial heritage.
>
> Louise migrated to the Northeast thirty years ago. She came at a time when industrial work was available and has spent about half of her life in manufacturing jobs [eventually acquiring] a college education ... She has experienced herself as rejected by her siblings and her mother because of her "book knowledge." As a result, Louise has limited her achievement and her income. Some of her resistance to embracing a middle-class lifestyle has been derived from an unconscious fear of loss of black identity and a greater loss of family. Louise has made a conscious effort to maintain a working-class identification even though her family values are middle-class. Her strong identification with the underprivileged has helped her performance at work where she has successfully articulated the needs of her poorest clients. (p. 134)

Louise's fear of success is accompanied by her life-long sense of unattractiveness. Her ego ideal of black attractiveness consists of almond-colored skin, European features, and straight or wavy hair—features which two of her sisters have. But as therapy progressed it turns out that valued family features of attractiveness, intelligence, and success cover up deeper and more destructive family dynamics, chief of which is her mother's declaring her unattractive because of her outspoken criticism of the family myths and emotionally siding with her father.

> Louise's basic resistance to defining herself as an educated, self-sufficient, and socially mobile Black woman is multi-determined. First, she fears that achieving more than her family would leave her even more alienated. Second, true self-sufficiency would eliminate the minimal feelings she has about her femininity. Finally, her capacity to speak for and to identify with the underprivileged is tied to her maintenance of an identity within the group. These issues remain the most significant foci of Louise's continued treatment and serve as graphic examples of the complex interaction of racial, gender, class, and interpersonal factors that can be involved in the self-definition of many women of color.... (p. 135)

To me, Thompson's description of Louise illustrates how many ghosts—personal, positional, and transgenerational internalizations—often operate to limit self-definition and personal identity development.

Ahnna: "An International Adoption" —Eliana Gill[13]

Little is known of Ahnna's life in China before she was adopted and brought to the United States. Her mother had died in childbirth and her father didn't want to care for her because he blamed her for his wife's death. The maternal grandmother cared for her until she was a year and a half when her grandmother died of cancer and Ahnna was placed in an orphanage.

---

[13] Gill, E. "From Sensitivity to Competence in Working across Cultures." In E. Gill & A. A. Drewes. (2005). *Cultural Issues in Play Therapy.* New York: The Guildford Press.

Scott and Joelle were college sweethearts from the Midwest before they were married and took positions in the East. After discovering their infertility they spent three years waiting on adoption lists before traveling to China. They chose Ahnna to adopt because of her compliant behavior and sweet appearance.

> A few months after the adoption, Scott and Joelle brought Ahnna to therapy because she was smearing feces, wetting the bed at night, hitting other children in kindergarten, whining and complaining of stomachaches, and becoming aggressive with the family dog. Ahnna was also masturbating in her bed, distressing both her parents, who panicked that this suggested that Ahnna had been sexually abused. They were distraught, weary, and desperate. Their dreams of a happy family had dissipated into a sea of distress. Although they had anticipated some difficulties with the child, they were shocked and somewhat disgusted with Ahnna's behavior. Their expectations were gravely challenged, and they felt incompetent and ashamed. (p. 4)

The psychosocial history of the adoptive parents proved unremarkable in that both were from large, loving, intact middle-class families, and both were in good mental and physical health. When they discovered they were unable to have children they heard that Chinese and Russian babies were easiest to obtain at that time. The parent's expressed no concern regarding race or culture, Ahnna was a beautiful child and that was what mattered.

Gill details the personal work she herself did in preparation for working with this family. She spent time attempting to visualize what each of the lives of both parents and what the life of Ahnna had been like prior to the adoption. She had worked on a number of international adoptions but the unique circumstances and cultural orientations of this family required careful consideration. Further, Gill describes the work she did in an effort to increase her depth of understanding of China and the Chinese cultural roots of Ahnna. At the first therapy session Ahnna initially had a hard time separating from her mother but when she discovered the sand tray she was delighted and created a world with a circle of Chinese dragons, two masks, and some lovely pale crystals.

> The next time Ahnna came, she made a beeline to the sandbox and proceeded to take out the Chinese dragons, masks, and pale crystals. This time she surrounded one of the masks in red crystals and placed it diagonally across from the other mask. She then put green trees (later, stones) around the second mask and drew lines with her finger in the center of the tray, making a sign. I was intrigued by the sign, and went to the Internet to look up Chinese letters and symbols. I was interested to find that she had drawn the symbol for "mother" between the two masks. The dragons were placed in dyads around the tray. (p. 15)

In subsequent sessions Ahnna chose to bathe and dress the baby—Chinese pajamas for sleeping and Western clothes for eating or going out. By the end of therapy she was dressing the doll in only Chinese clothes. Joelle had purchased her Chinese clothes which she alternately wore as she chose. Gill describes many moving moments with Ahnna in therapy as she drew family pictures and colored herself brown and her parents pink. They matched pencils and hands and worked on all sorts of troubling situations in the sand. Gill met monthly with Scott and Joelle, coaching them to accept her regressive behaviors as part of a transition and teaching them how to distract, comfort, and guide Ahnna.

> As Ahnna developed a new expressive strategy in therapy—namely, "playing it out"—her behavioral problems decreased accordingly. In addition, Scott and Joelle quickly learned that their parenting strategies could help increase or decrease the problem behaviors. Their insights and willingness to follow advice and then generate their own creative interventions made working with this couple a delight. (p. 18)

Gill counseled the parents on bedtime routines, limit setting, baths, and book reading—especially those that highlighted ethnic differences. Scott and Joelle were at first ethnically blind and had to be educated to how much nuances of difference mattered to Ahnna. Once they caught onto the importance of understanding difference, they hired a Chinese tutor to help Ahnna hold on to the Chinese language and to be an ethnic role model. They learned the Chinese holidays and how to celebrate them with her. Gill also encouraged them to give her knowledge about the Midwest and the families and cultural milieu to which they would soon return.

> Scott and Joelle kept in touch after therapy ended, giving me progress reports. Ahnna had become the apple of their eye, and they looked back with amazement at the acute difficulties they had experienced after Ahnna first arrived in the United States. They eventually moved back to their Midwestern hometown, and left the East Coast with a strong resolve to approach their families of origin with all the information they had acquired about China, true biculturalism, and acculturation. (p. 19)

In my experience, altogether too often the "melting pot" approach is taken to cross-cultural and cross-racial adoptions—rather than the "mosaic" approach. That is, adoptive parents in their eagerness to ensure acceptance are frequently insensitive to the need to help their adoptive children define and come to grips with racial, ethnic, linguistic, cultural, and national differences. This case serves for me as an ideal example of how parents can develop such sensitivities and thereby promote rich personal identities.

Part III:
Depth Psychological Understanding in Cross-Cultural Contexts

Marius: "Eskimo PTSD"—Peter Levine[14]

One of the most moving cross-cultural encounters in the psychotherapy literature is told by body psychotherapist Peter Levine. There are more than forty schools of body psychotherapy in the United States—each having developed techniques for accessing psychological constellations through attention to various parts of the body and the body's energies. Typically body therapy is taught in groups of therapists that convene periodically to witness experts work with someone in their group on releasing pent-up tensions of one kind or another. This event occurred in a training session in Copenhagen, Denmark between Levine and a young "Eskimo" described as intelligent, shy, slight in his mid-twenties from a small village in Greenland.

Marius begins his work with Levine by reporting his periodic bouts of anxiety and panic, notably when he is with a man whose approval he desires. During these moments he experiences weak legs and a stabbing pain on the side of his right leg. In telling this to Levine he suddenly experiences his face as warm, sweaty and flushed. He is reminded of an event that happened before he was eight years old. Marius was returning home from a walk in the mountains when he was attacked by a pack of three wild dogs and bitten badly on his right leg. He remembers the bite and waking up in the arms of a neighbor who was carrying him home. He recalls his father coming to the door and being annoyed. Marius reports having felt bitter, angry, and hurt by his father's rejection. His new polar bear fur pants his mother had just made for him were all ripped and covered with blood. As he talks to Levine his demeanor

---

[14] Levine, P. & Frederick, A. (1997). *Waking the Tiger: Healing Trauma: The Innate Capacity to Transform Overwhelming Experiences.* North Atlantic Books.

switches to pleasure and pride in telling him about the fur pants his mother had made especially for him. He excitedly holds his hands in front of him as though feeling the fur and its soft warmth. These pants were like the grown men of the village wore to hunt. His excitement increases as he imagines feeling the pants in his hands. Levine asks him to feel the legs inside his pants. As Mario feels his legs, he reports that his legs feel strong. He imagines seeing a large expanse of rocks. He wants to jump up and down on the rocks. His legs feel light and strong now, like springs. A long stick suddenly appears beside the rocks—it's a spear, and he picks it up.

> "I am following a large polar bear. I am with the men, but I will make the kill." (Very small movements can be seen in his thigh, pelvic, and trunk muscles, as he imagines jumping from rock to rock in following the trail.) "I see him now. I stop and aim my spear."
>
> "Yes," I say, "Feel that in your whole body, feel your feet on the rocks, the strength in your legs, and the arching in your back and arms, feel all that power."
>
> "I see the spear flying," he says. Again, small postural adjustments can be seen in Marius' body; he is trembling lightly now in his legs and arms. I encourage him to feel these sensations. He reports waves of excitement and pleasure. "I did it. I hit him with my spear!"

As Marius' fantasy unfolds the men cut the belly of the bear open, take out the insides, cut up the meat for food in the village, and cut up the fur to make pants and coats.

> "Feel your pants, Marius, with your hands on your legs."...Tears form in his eyes. "Can you do this?" [kill

and skin a bear] I ask. "I don't know...I'm scared." "Feel your legs, feel your pants." He shouts in Eskimo, dramatically, in an increasing pitch. "...Yes, I cut the belly open, there is lots of blood...I take out the insides. Now I cut the skin, I rip it off, there is glistening and shimmering. It is a beautiful fur, thick and soft. It will be very warm."

Throughout the telling Marius' body builds with tremors of excitement, strength, and courage. The total bodily arousal is intense and visible. When Levine asks how he feels, Marius reports being a little scared but very strong, maybe stronger than he's ever felt. He says feeling strong is okay now—he's feeling powerful and filled with energy. He worries a little, but he thinks he can trust the strong feelings he is experiencing. Levine encourages Marius to take his time, to feel his strength, and to touch his legs and feet.

"Now start walking down, back towards the village." (I am directing the newly resourced man towards the traumatic moment.) A few minutes pass, then Marius' trunk flexes and he holds still. His heart rate accelerates, and his face reddens. "I see the dogs...they're coming at me." "Feel your legs, Marius, touch the pants," I demand sharply. "Feel your legs and look. What is happening?" "I am turning, turning away. I see the dogs. I see a pole, an electricity pole. I am turning towards it. I didn't know that I remembered this." Marius pales. "I'm getting weak." "Feel the pants, Marius," I command, "feel the pants with your hands." "I'm running." His color returns. "I can feel my legs...they're strong, like on the rocks." Again he pales and yells out: "Agh!...my leg, it burns like fire...I can't move, I'm trying, but I can't move...I can't...I can't move, it's numb now...my leg is numb, I can't feel it." "Turn, Marius. Turn to the dog. Look at it."... I hand Marius a roll of paper towels.... He grabs the roll and strangles it as the other group members, myself included, look on with utter amazement at his strength as he twists it and almost tears it in two. "Now the other one, look right at it...look right in its eyes." This time he lets out screams of rage and triumph.

Levine allows Marius to settle a bit before asking what he sees now. "I see them...they're all bloody and dead." As he calms, he turns his head to the right and Levine asks him what he sees now. He sees the telephone pole with bolts in it and runs toward it. "I am running...I can feel my legs, they're strong like springs.... I'm climbing...climbing...I see them below... they're dead and I'm safe." He starts to sob softly.

As Marius breathing and body undulations settle down he feels himself being carried by strong arms of the neighbor man, passing fences and houses in the village. "He's knocking at the door of my family's house. The door opens...my father...he's very upset, he runs to get a towel...my leg is bleeding badly...my pants are torn...he's very upset...he's not mad at me, he's very worried. It hurts, the soap hurts." Marius sobs now in full, gentle waves. "It hurts. But I'm crying 'cause he's not angry at me... I can see he was upset and scared. I feel vibration and tingling all over, it's even and warm.... He loves me."

Moments later Marius reports being okay—warm and peaceful. He says he now realizes that his father was just scared, not that his father doesn't love him.

Levine sees Marius' healing journey as a mythic one known to us all from childhood traumas. Healing ourselves is heroic with moments of brilliance, learning and hard work. Sometimes the healing is suddenly like with Marius in a single session, but usually healing is more open-ended, occurring gradually over time.

Maria: Being Enveloped and Suffocated by Slime
—Miguel Reyes[15]

Several years ago I was preparing a book, *Terrifying Transferences: Aftershocks of Childhood Trauma*, to illustrate how primitive terror can be projected into the therapist in various ways. The purpose of the book was to encourage therapists to tune into their own puzzling emotional responses to clients in order to learn more about their client's inner lives. I put out a call to colleagues to contribute clinical experiences illustrating how they had learned about their clients by paying attention to their own strange feelings in connection with their clients.

Psychologist John Carter was supervising the psychotherapy work of psychologist Miguel Reyes, with a young Hispanic woman in a community clinic. While both client and therapist were of Hispanic extraction they were culturally very different, and they very different from John and myself as Anglos. We three met with the tape recorder going in an attempt to puzzle out what might be going on with the strange emotional experiences Miguel was having in response to Maria. The purpose of excerpting this lengthy study here is to show that despite a variety of complex cultural and socio-economic variables as well as a host of alienating psychodynamics at play, Miguel and Maria's work together was able to bridge a seemingly unbridgeable gap. Here are some transcribed notes from our session together:

---

[15] From Hedges, L. E. (1996). *Terrifying Transferences: Aftershocks of Childhood Trauma*. New Jersey: Aronson

Miguel: This couple, Maria and Arturo, is intriguing because although I had been working with them for over a year, I still had not been able to understand the particular transferences and countertransferences operating. But the couple recently separated. And that's when I first got a glimmer of what had been going on. The best thing I can say to start with is that the transference felt "splashy," "gooey," and that it left me with a feeling of slime or filthiness. I know this is a strange description of countertransference feelings but...

Larry: It is strange...

Miguel: It was like some kind of slimy feeling that I would clean myself from after sessions, but I could never quite understand what it was about. I would leave the session feeling like, well, the sexual image that comes to my mind is someone ejaculating all over me, smearing me with it, and my not liking it.

Larry: This is strange.

Miguel: That dirty, slimy feeling was disturbing and confounding to me, until recently when Maria separated from Arturo. It finally came out that he had been screwing other women behind her back. And It was almost as if she had been carrying his raging, or his rageful ejaculatory processes for a long time. And that the rageful, sexual sliming was being somehow transmitted to me, through her. That's the feeling of it.

John: Didn't you say at one time that Arturo acted as a pimp and prostituted her in some way?

Miguel: Yes he did.

Larry: This is an amazing beginning, because what you're saying is that the sexual processes here are being used really for some kind of gruesome hostile purpose.

Miguel: Yes. Gruesome hostile purpose, exactly.

Larry: And that some of this primitive, hostile sexuality has been directed at you. That's the feeling that you've been having?

Miguel: I know it's strange, but yes. I went fifteen sessions with this couple until they divulged that when they first got married, they had no money so she went off and worked as a prostitute. He managed her, allowed her to do it, and sold her. But in retrospect I'm not so sure the pimping and prostitution was only for money. There was something really disgusting about it all. Behind it was driving rage and terror.

Larry: We might not always find prostitution disgusting. But there was something about it in this case that you found totally disgusting?

Miguel: It was degrading, that's why. It was forced upon her out of rage with humiliating intentions. And there was some deep unidentified element of terror.

Larry: I'm thinking, for example, that we might find someone raised in a barrio and living in desperate conditions finding some meaningful sense of self through prostitution. Or engaging in sex for money out of necessity of for some other important purpose.

Miguel: Yes.

Larry: So we could imagine many reasons for prostitution which might have some redeeming value to the self or to life—given certain circumstances. But here you're saying we have degradation, force, humiliation, rage, and fear.

Miguel: Yes, there was a degrading quality to all of their sex like it was done more out of anger and fear. It was like his saying "Fuck you," and "I will screw you over good." And her feeling some terror and a need to submit. But a year later when Maria later separated from Arturo, that slimy quality stopped. It was almost as if she were a vehicle, a carrier of his rageful degrading transference, or whatever he was projecting. And it was landing on me.

Larry: The disgusting, degrading, dominating, slimy, transference was aimed at you. It had a "fuck you" quality, aimed squarely at you?

Miguel: Aimed at me, channeled through her.

Larry: Your body language shows us not only facial disgust, but a sense of your skin crawling.

Miguel: Yes. Some sense of dirt, slime, ooze, splash—"get off of me." When much later Maria broke off the relationship with him, things were suddenly cleaner. I was suddenly cleaner. I didn't feel slimed on by a disgusting pimp.

Larry: An awesome beginning.

Miguel: I thought a description of those strange feelings might help clarify something of the nature of their relationship.

Larry: Yes.

Miguel: Arturo refused to continue therapy on a regular basis after the fifteenth session because he was angry at her. After their disclosure to me of their pimp/prostitute activities he became very mistrustful towards her. He felt that she was going to go out and continue using her body as a prostitute behind his back. That was his constant complaint. But though he stopped attending regular sessions, she continued to. That's when I really started sensing this slimy, gooey, repulsive feeling like someone was ejaculating all over me. I couldn't define the feeling very well until she left him and then it was like I wasn't weighed down any more with trying to clean myself off all the time. It was like I didn't have to waste my energy dodging the slime. I was able to talk more freely. During the time when the oppressive transference projection was occurring, a lot of my energies were directed towards cleaning myself off, cleaning the mess up. I can't tell you how, it's just the feeling.

Larry: Well, here again, we can imagine a variety of circumstances, in which we might think of sexual juices, ejaculation, and so forth, being on us in ways that could be interesting, exciting, and even beautiful.

Miguel: Yes.

Larry: And yet, there's something here about it; that is, the essence of love itself, is being used to smear you. That's the feeling.

Miguel: That was the feeling. It was smearing, their juices being used to smear me. I was once working in a special school setting with a child who enjoyed smearing his feces over the bathroom wall. This had that over-the-edge quality to it. In the case with the child he was very hostile, very angry, rageful towards his mom. It was almost as if he were smearing feces on the mom. Something about coloring someone up or smearing somebody over with one's body fluids. Like there's some kind of perverse hostile goal there. Like there's a gain in doing that.

John: I believe you once said "mar."

Miguel: You mar them, yes.

Larry: You've used the word "slimed" several times.

Miguel: Yes. There was a distorting of my image. A marring of her image, a marring of my image.

John: I am associating to about fifteen or so years ago. Some guy in Italy hit the Pieta, you know the Michelangelo statue of Mary holding Jesus. He hit it, I think with a small hammer. He was trying to mar or deface this symbol that is traditionally beautiful and significant.

Larry: Deface it. Deface Maria.

John: Yes. Deface it. Deface her–Maria, exactly.

Miguel: Yes. It felt like a defacing. It's like spilling paint over a sacred statue. This particular man was originally from Argentina. And now that I think about it, if I'm not mistaken, it's by no means uncommon in that culture to deface symbols that represent authority you are disgusted with, that you do not like. You deface it by painting, you pour paint over it and discolor it, distort it, deface it, mar the image.

Larry: Well, Miguel, tell us about the case.

Miguel: What would you like to know?

Larry: How did it start? How did it go? How did all this awful feeling develop?

Miguel: The feeling emerged slowly after the fifteenth session when they both divulged this secret. Obviously there was a lot of shame around it. She had agreed to provide the money to pay for food and rent, and he had sold her, degraded her, defaced her.

Larry: On the surface the shame is because they had done something bad or wrong, but on a deeper level...

Miguel: Exactly. On a deeper level the profound sense of shame may have meant many things. They both felt the shame. She felt the shame afterwards, in that she had done it. And he felt the shame for allowing her to do it. There had been a collusion, a shameful one. They both felt the shame, and they kept it inside for fifteen sessions. All of a sudden it came out, just before they ran off on a vacation. When they returned, she came in alone. She wanted to continue therapy, he didn't. She wasn't clear as to why he didn't want to come back. I had him come in once or twice and I did talk to him. He was very passive-aggressive. He couldn't exactly tell me why he didn't want to continue. But strikingly, when she starting coming in on her own, she started dressing very provocatively.

Larry: Distinctly differently from the way she had dressed before?

Miguel: Oh yes. She came in with miniskirts more often, frilly blouses, short belly shirts. I felt like there was some sexualization of our process going on. As though perhaps she were prostituting again. Almost as if she were being sent in by the pimp. Like some aggressive intent was being lived out through her which was affecting not only her but me. I didn't feel slimed immediately. I didn't take off on the slime feeling until probably the second or third session with her alone.

Larry: You had not felt the negative intent in the first fifteen sessions?

Miguel: No. There was actually a nice collaborative sense among the three of us. We worked well on communication issues.

Larry: You haven't told us yet why they came, or how divulging the secret of the prostitution happened.

Miguel: Yes. Well, the presenting problem was that they were in warfare about communications, they both complained about not being able to communicate.

Larry: How long had they been together?

Miguel: Three or four years. They wanted to work on better communication. Specifically, she complained about him being overly dependent on her. She felt very suffocated, engulfed by him, dominated by his dependency. He complained about feeling that she didn't care about his, um, what was the way he said it, "She doesn't help me feel important." She complained about feeling engulfed by his demands. But at the same time, it was as if she were inviting that engulfment. She wanted the mental-physical fusion. But then she complained about the stifling, suffocating effects of the fusion.

Larry: When you moved into Spanish, the implication becomes more passive than it is in English, doesn't it? We can say she doesn't make me feel important, but it doesn't quite carry the same passivity that it does in the Spanish, *Ella no me hace sentir importante*?

Miguel: No, it doesn't.

Larry: Spanish uses the reflexive. Like it's her job to make me or help me feel important.

Miguel: Yes. Maria complained about the dependent fusion, but then she wanted, she invited the fusion. And then Arturo complained that she was making him feel unimportant. Much of this came through glimpses of their sex life. There was no problem with their sex life.

Larry: You mean no problem in the sense that it was active and alive.

Miguel: Yes. Active, alive, and fulfilling as sex. There was plenty of sexual, physical intimacy.

Larry: They were together three or four years. Were they married during this time period?

Miguel: Three years married, the first year they lived together.

Larry: And the prostitution occurred during that first year?

Miguel: It occurred towards the end of that first year just before getting married.

Larry: And how had their economic situation shifted by the time they started seeing you? There had been difficulties in the beginning?

Miguel: Arturo had received some kind of compensation, through a lawsuit or something to that effect. So they had a large sum of money, and they were able to use that. And Maria was working as a massage therapist.

Larry: Body work. Did he work at all?

Miguel: He was working in construction.

Larry: So they were doing much better economically at the time that they came to you?

Miguel: Right, yes. But physically there were problems. This is one couple that skin contact was very important to. Skin contact is very important for her. It is like she knows that she exists through some type of tactile sensory process. She needs the skin contact. He does too. Very much so. Both of them have some desperation for skin contact. I'm sure that's why sex was so frequent and so lively.

Larry: In the countertransference, your images are tactile about ejaculation, slime, dirt all over you. These are skin sensations. So it is almost like in the counter-transference you felt the hostility being projected at the skin level.

Miguel: I hadn't thought of that, but it's true.

Larry: You didn't tell us, for example, that your stomach turned or your heart was racing, or your feet were cold...

Miguel: No. The feelings definitely had a tactile reference. Now, while she was still with him but coming to therapy by herself, she dressed provocatively. It was as if some sexualization of her surface were going on.

Larry: There again she is showing skin.

Miguel: Yes, she is showing plenty of skin, plenty of skin.

Larry: And, let's face it, invading your boundaries that way.

Miguel: Invading my boundaries?

Larry: Sure. A female client comes to a male therapist in a professional environment and gives him lots of skin. It is a kind of violation. You are not there to look at, to be entertained by her skin.

Miguel: That is true. She is bringing up my awareness of her skin, but she is not bringing up much about herself.

Larry: This is different than somebody coming in their sweats or shorts from the gym. But even there you don't necessarily show skin. She is deliberately showing skin.

Miguel: Then all of a sudden this is when we started experiencing troubles. It could be that he was disapproving of her coming to see me. On the one hand sending her alone; but on the other resenting her seeing me, provoking me. Like he was playing off of the theme of feeling important. He wasn't feeling important by her coming to therapy on her own. But he didn't choose to come in with her.

Larry: He's either knowing that she wanted to seduce you. Or he's knowingly sending her to seduce you, to have a skin relationship with you–all the while feeling neglected or unimportant.

Miguel: Yes. So he gave her his rage, projecting it into her through their primitive skin, ejaculatory contact processes. It occurs to me smearing ejaculation could easily have been a part of their hostile sexuality. That would certainly fit–skin hunger, ravaging, whatever.

John: Were you important? Is she making you important by going to therapy?

Miguel: Yes.

John: But if you are slimed, then you are not so important anymore? If I deface you then you are not important? If I depersonalize you?

Larry: We are certainly asking a lot of weird questions here.

John: We certainly are. That's why we wanted to go over this case with you together. This is all so fused and confused–so sticky and icky we can't tell who's doing what to whom

Larry: But it is interesting, Miguel, that you are suggesting that in some perverse way a third party may be an essential aspect to their deeper, but disturbing sexual urges. That he is using her to express his hostility/sexuality toward you, almost in a homosexual way.

Miguel: Yes. So I continue probing, just continue to probe not being able to make much sense of anything that's going on of what I'm feeling. I don't think she knew what she was doing consciously. She may have sensed that she was a carrier of his rageful, defacing projective identification. Because surely there was a place in her that was compliant, that found this position somehow familiar. And, now that you mention it, it is interesting that I characterize my own activities at this point as probing.

Larry: Let me ask you a cross-cultural question here. I am well aware that among Latinas there is a greater tendency to show skin in mini-skirts, belly blouses, and so forth–say more than there might be in the Anglo culture. What is your feeling here?

Miguel: Good question. Because I have other female clients, Latinas who come in, showing plenty of skin, but there isn't that sense of sexualization, of provocativeness, of seduction.

Larry: So her skin was highly eroticized and you felt it?

Miguel: Yes. I felt it, I certainly did. I mean, I have had other clients who come in wearing mini-skirts and belly shirts; but there isn't that energy of sexualization in it all.

John: Even I felt it that time I accidentally ran into her in the hall at our clinic. I was coming back from the restroom one day when she was leaving the building. Afterward I ran into Miguel in the staff room...

Miguel: He knew it was her from my description of my feelings.

John: I knew by the way her skin was eroticized. I didn't feel the seduction, but I felt the eroticization of the skin. And the way she walked. She looked over at me not seductively. But her skin was alive, her skin was alive, vibrant, eroticized. I don't know how to describe it but it truly was.

Larry: So you do make a distinction about the way she carries herself and other Latinas who may also show skin as a part of a cultural feature?

Miguel: Right. When I meet with other Latinas who show skin, there isn't that charged quality. It seemed almost with her that I sense her skin trying to envelop me, trying to cover me, trying to reach out to me, to come upon me, to cover me over. With other women I don't feel that enveloping sense. Their skin, their beauty is just there–a part of them. That is who they are and they are retaining their skin. Keeping inside of their own bodies. Here she is giving away her skin. There is the distinction, other Latinas can retain their skin. With her it is different. It is like she–really both of them–are putting it on you for the purpose of knowing something about themselves or you. Funny image–not retaining your own skin but aggressively engulfing someone else with it.

Larry: Like some sort of an invasion.

Miguel: It is an invasion. And with it a quality of suffocation.

Larry: Suffocation?

Miguel: Yes. It is almost like putting saran wrap, cellophane wrap around your head and you are trying to breathe with it on. The texture is all over you. You are trying to breathe. I am really going into this now because of what I am sensing as we talk. I have been trying to understand these feelings for a long time and that is what I have been feeling. It is like a cellophane wrap being wrapped around me and it is a skin-to-skin pressure–a tactile, sensory process and it is suffocating to me because it is wrapped around my face. But, prior to her breaking up with her boyfriend, her husband, that tactile quality of wrapping around me somehow involved what I eventually came to call the skin with smeared semen. Could it be that in his rage he smeared her skin with his rageful semen, and I picked up on that because of her trying to envelop me with her skin which was already smeared with his rageful semen? Like it was inevitable that I feel his rageful semen because of her process of always trying to envelop people, me, with her skin?

Larry: It's a three-way somehow and you are feeling used, your presence is somehow important to who they are together.

Miguel: Making me important, yes.

Larry: We have to figure out "important" in what sense. As a third person, a love object, or as a fetish?

Miguel: Well, she is going to another guy for a relationship.

John: Yes, and it is intimate.

Miguel: For self-fulfillment. For a relationship, perhaps for orgasm. He complains she is prostituting herself with other guys but she denies it.

Larry: So he sends her, but then we feel his rage.

Miguel: But we haven't addressed the homosexual thread yet. In the first fifteen sessions he expressed a deep appreciation for my help. I mean there was a level of genuiness in his expressions of appreciation. There had been something upsetting that happened when they had visited her family in Colombia. He was deeply grateful for my help in sorting all of that out. It had been important. Maybe that developed some level of attachment with him where I became like a mother transference object to him. Because he really opened up. He cried. He let himself feel deeply in the short time we had together–which I found remarkable for a man who was very invested in machismo.

Larry: So the homosexual thread is really more of a deep maternal attachment?

Miguel: Yes. I would say it is a dependent maternal attachment.

Larry: So possibly mother's body is being assaulted with his body products? Yours is.

Miguel: Yes.

Larry: And there is your association to the little boy smearing feces who is angry with his mother.

Miguel: After the fifteenth session comes a month or so off, a vacation and few phone calls from her. She is eager to come in, to see me. I tell her I want her to come in. I want to see them both.

Larry: What were those sessions actually like?

Miguel: Okay. The sessions, well, on several occasions she would walk in and immediately shake my hand and kiss me on the cheek. An invasion. You're right, a skin invasion.

Larry: This is not just a friendly Latina greeting? This is more an invasion?

Miguel: It is an invasion.

Larry: Okay.

Miguel: During the first fifteen sessions she had greeted me with a Hispanic handshake and a kiss twice but it was different. Now the greeting takes on a different quality that made me feel uncomfortable. It was sexualized. It was excessive. It was more in tune with the skin. Suffocating. It was like the cellophane wrap on my head.

Larry: So she shakes your hand and kisses you on the cheek. But you want to pull back.

Miguel: And then she starts complaining. She did a lot of splitting–seeing her husband as all bad. In contrast, she was very solicitous toward me, always complimenting me on how nice I was, how I have helped her a lot, what a nice person I am, or how she liked a particular shirt I was wearing. I felt over-idealized by her. She was putting me on a pedestal. All the while denigrating, devaluing Arturo. She was very childlike in her neediness as though she were very dependent on me. She would always say, "Oh, I don't think I could ever make it without you. You are the only one who listens to me." It was excessive, it was over-idealizing, and it was suffocating too.

Larry: One great way to ensure no real contact in a relationship is by excessively praising the other. It always alienates.

Miguel: Yes. All this verbiage on her part was suffocating. It was like, I didn't feel like I was Miguel. I didn't feel like she was relating to me. I thought, "Who is she relating to?" It was like I wasn't there at times in the session. You're right, it's like I was some sort of idealized fetish.

Larry: Was she using the sessions to solicit advice and help or more just to pour out her woes and seduce you?

Miguel: She was trying to use me to give her quick answers to her problems. I kept trying to take her back to her pain. And, she would cry for a brief moment and then jump on the idealization track again.

Larry: So you really never had hold of her?

Miguel: No, I never had hold of her. She seemed to slip through my fingers–so to speak!

Larry: I have a question since we have here an erotic transference of sorts. We live in a day now where we are paranoid about sex in therapy and therapists being accused of sexual encounters. Was there ever any sense of her trying to engage you sexually or did this really stay more at the level of this deep, destructive slime and invasion?

Miguel: It stayed at the level of that deep, destructive slime, that invasion. Come to think of it though, there was a moment in which it was almost as if she were inviting me to go between her legs.

Larry: Can you tell us about that moment?

Miguel: There was a session where she started idealizing me. But the idealizing was such it was almost like she was inviting, "have sex with me, come alongside of me, come inside." That was the implication to the nature of our talk. The way she was idealizing me and how I get her to talk. Like it would be really great being intimate with me. Maybe the "inside her, between her legs" is more my material in response to her. She was giving me skin, she wanted skin fusion with me, and there was a point in that process where she wanted fusion in a sexual sense, but a fusion that defaces, depersonalizes, suffocates me. Perhaps this all goes back to her father, if you look at her developmental history. She had a very close, fused but unsatisfactory relationship with her father. She was emotionally incested.

Larry: But not, so far as you know, physically?

Miguel: Not so far as I know. She never acknowledged anything like that. But there was a lot of emotional incest. He used her as a surrogate spouse and as a source of emotional containment. It could have been skin again, closeness, sensual, sexual I suppose.

Larry: So this whole question of being given away to another to be used, which comes up in the relationship with her husband, is a long-standing theme for her as well. Her mother gave her away to her father who fused with her in some primitive, sensual, erotic way. And she is now being given away to you.

Miguel: Yes. There is a theme of her wanting to fuse with Dad— but there was an unsatisfactory attachment with her father. It is as if she were somehow trying to accomplish that same sense with me in therapy. And with other men in general by giving away her skin. That is the way she knows she exists, that's the way she knows she is important. That is herself. Her identity involves her enveloping, containing a man–or someone. That is her source of existence–fusing with the other.

Larry: So go ahead, you saw her for this period and then we have a break up in the relationship don't we? How long a period after they came back from vacation before they broke up?

Miguel: I would say eight to twelve weeks. They made a mutual decision to leave each other. Now through that eight- to twelve-week period Arturo did come in a couple sessions. I was trying to get him engaged again in the couples therapy process.

Larry: Because you could see their relationship was in trouble?

Miguel: Yes. I told Maria that it would be best if we meet as a couple again because of the nature of the problem. Since it was relational, since we were talking about marital issues.

Larry: You are smiling a bit. Are you trying to tell us also that in the countertransference you felt some awkwardness with the seduction, or...?

Miguel: Well, I started panicking.

Larry: Panicking, because?

Miguel: I felt panicky because I didn't want this to go anywhere, to get out of hand.

Larry: The sexual seduction?

Miguel: Right. Knowing her fundamental lack of reality testing, I felt that she could easily distort the therapeutic relationship to possibly mean something else in her need for intimate fusion and her over idealization of me. So I thought I better keep a check on this by seeing if her husband could be a part of the process too.

Larry: What were you afraid of?

Miguel: I was afraid of being accused of misleading her. I was afraid of her distorting the relationship. And I was afraid of her marring my image.

Larry: With him, the world, your wife, what?

Miguel: Yes. At all those levels I suppose, my wife, the world, as a professional, as an individual, and as a therapist. By getting him back into session I was trying to protect my image. To prevent it from being marred by her delusional process. I was trying to preserve myself. So we go back to the marring of image.

Larry: From your physical discomfort here, it is like it hit a deep level, this fear.

Miguel: Yes. Let me give some background. They first came to know me through a workshop I conducted at a large local church. So I have a public and professional image at stake.

Larry: So in the broader community in which you live and practice if Maria revives this incest experience from her childhood, transfers it to you, and somehow accuses you of some sort of impropriety, then you are not so much worried about him coming and killing you as you are about some sort of discrediting, defacing exposure in the community? A third party again is the source of danger somehow.

Miguel: Yes. I am not as worried about Arturo as I am worried about my image in the community being marred by her distortions of me.

Larry: You have assessed that both of them have a reality testing problem of sorts in their dependent fusing dynamics, so there is a psychotic process here in both members of the couple, and probably going on between them. So you have not only a countertransferential fear of close contact but a realistic one as well?

Miguel: Yes, I sensed there was a psychotic process operating in subtle ways. I felt a need to firmly set the boundaries. I told her that I would continue seeing her in the context of marriage because the nature of the problem was essentially marital. I was firm in telling her that we needed to go back to the problem of communication.

Larry: But in holding the boundaries regarding the couples aspect, you were also implicitly refusing the seduction, the transference role being assigned you as the fetish object of the fusion, of the object of perverse hostile envelopment.

Miguel: Yes. So I finally got Arturo to come in for several sessions. He was accusing her of whoring around. Recall, she lived with her dad growing up, her mom wasn't around. I know little of the early mothering process. As you say, her mother gave her away to her father. There was an aunt who was basically her maternal figure. Her aunt repeatedly accused Maria of being a "puta" (a whore). And basically that is what he was doing to her in the session. You are becoming a puta, you are acting like a whore.

Larry: So the skin invasion that you felt so very clearly has been operating throughout her life. And her aunt picked up on it early on. Arturo is using it to abuse her in front of you.

Miguel: Oh yes. And come to think of it, it is a skin invasion designed to tantalize and tease.

John: I have been having this thought that in a sense that is what father did. Father invades with all his seductive treatment of her, his using her for whatever his dependent merger needs were. He invaded her with his own emotional needs and with his verbal or emotional sexualizing during her growing up years. So she married somebody who does a similar thing to her. And you feel endangered by that transference with an invasive, boundaryless, psychotic core.

Miguel: That seems right. Scary, isn't it?

Larry: Where else do you want to go with this, Miguel?

Miguel: After the separation all the provocativeness, all of the sexualization, all of that skin contact, and all that slimy, gooey stuff stopped.

Larry: The acting out of the primitive three-way ceased. And she had gotten your message about professional boundaries. So what has this last round of therapy been like then?

Miguel: This last round of therapy has been the most productive. We are getting someplace now.

John: In what way?

Miguel: I don't feel invaded. She respects my space. I don't feel I need to protect my image, conserve my image, save face. There is not that concern about being marred, slimed upon, or defaced. The deep unnameable dread or terror has completely disappeared.

Larry: What is she working on?

Miguel: She is working on defining what part of her true self is putting that skin erotization, envelopment on other people because she has a deep need for contact. But she senses that her ways of going for it are somehow not working for her.

Larry: So the idea of her coming off like a whore is part of what she is trying to come to grips with?

Miguel: Yes. She is accepting that and seeing that it extends from an inner need.

Larry: And how does she formulate that need?

Miguel: Well, she is starting to connect that with her need for fathering. She is looking to attach to a father figure who will respect her body.

Larry: And it sounds like she's getting that with you. But we are a long way from getting back to the early mother skin contact?

Miguel: Yes. I have no idea about her mother.

Larry: Except that we have to assume the hostile fusing, using transference/countertransference feelings are early memories of maternal contact.

John: She almost started believing in it, that the slimy, hostile part was her. Like seeing herself in a looking glass or...

Miguel: Well, in some sense she did believe it. She embodied it.

Larry: That's true. But you are saying that she is starting now in her therapy to get beneath that transference illusion to realize there is some desperate need at stake and she has gotten so far now as to relate it to her need for love from a respectful father. We haven't yet moved to the place where she is able to trace the perverse need for hostile skin contact back to her early mother experiences.

We have only five minutes more. Let me test your intuition, Miguel. As you follow her in therapy, where do you predict this is going to go in terms of the deep maternal? What is her need, her deepest need that she is going to be trying to work out with you?

Miguel: I think her deepest need is the opposite of what she is trying to do towards men.

Larry: Say it.

Miguel: She needs to be enveloped. She needs to be wrapped around. She needs to be held like a loving mother would a child. It is like she is rejecting the lack of envelopment by the other. She wants to be safely and enjoyably held.

John: She has been functioning on the object side of the self-object continuum. She can envelop others but she doesn't know how to be enveloped herself.

Larry: So in a way we might say that the reason that she has been able to slowly respond to you and to your efforts to contain her and to hold her is because the therapeutic offering really promises being held in that way, promises being safely and satisfyingly enveloped by care. You have been doing that to her.

Miguel: Yes. I have been. There is a strong texture to my holding. In fact, she is starting to see therapy as a home. She will say, "I am coming home now." Sometimes I greet her with, "*Bienvenida a tu casa*," welcome home. The home she is looking to house herself in, to be held in. That is the track we are on now.

Larry: That is where you are going. That is a good place to stop. Thanks for sharing this peculiar set of countertransference reactions with us. I wish we knew more of the dynamics of where the hostility originated from and how it has gotten perversely merged with the erotic. But what we can say is that it was serving to alienate you through provoking panic and fear.

Miguel: Yes, it certainly was.

Larry: *Buena suerte*, Miguel!

Miguel: *Gracias*!

Postscript:

In this clinical vignette we have at least five unique cultural orientations at work as two clients, a therapist, and two supervisors attempt to construct bridges of understanding that hopefully will facilitate Maria in finding her own home.

Lévi-Strauss on "How Symbols 'Hook Into' the Body" —Lawrence Hedges[16]

The French anthropologist Claude Lévi-Strauss (1949) in a chapter titled "The Effectiveness of Symbols," undertakes a penetrating definition of the psychotherapeutic task, revealing from an anthropological and sociological viewpoint the necessarily dual nature of the psychotherapeutic endeavor. Further, his analysis explains to the Western, science-oriented, mind the psychodynamics of traditional healing techniques.

---

[16] Hedges (1994).

Lévi-Strauss reviews the first available South American magico-religious text, an eighteen-page incantation obtained by the Cuna Indian, Guillermo Haya, from an elderly informant of his tribe (original source: Holmer & Wassen 1947). The purpose of the song is to facilitate unusually difficult childbirth. Its use is unusual since native women of Central and South America have easier deliveries than women of Western societies. The intervention of the shaman is thus rare and occurs only in the extreme case of failure to deliver and at the request of the midwife.

The song begins with the midwife's confusion over the pregnant woman's failure to deliver and describes her visit to the shaman and the latter's arrival in the hut of the laboring woman, with his fumigations of burnt cocoa-nibs, his invocations, and the making of nuchu, sacred figures or images carved from various prescribed kinds of wood that lend them their effectiveness. The carved nuchu represent tutelary spirits who become the shaman's assistants. He leads the nuchu to the abode of Muu (inside the woman's body). Muu is the goddess of fertility and is responsible for the formation of the fetus. Difficult childbirths occur when Muu has exceeded her functions and captured the purba or soul of the mother. The incantation thus expresses a quest for the lost soul of the mother, which will be restored after overcoming many obstacles. The shaman's saga will take the woman through a victory over wild beasts and finally through a great contest waged by the shaman and his tutelary spirits against Muu and her daughters. Once Muu has been defeated, the whereabouts of the soul of the ailing woman can be discovered and freed so the delivery can take place. The song ends with precautions that must be taken so that Muu cannot pursue her victors (an event that would result in infertility). The fight is not waged against Muu herself, who is indispensable to procreation, but against her abuses of power. After the epic saga, Muu asks the shaman when he will come to visit again, indicating the perennial nature of psychic conflict that can be expected to interfere with childbirth.

Lévi-Strauss comments that in order to perform his function the shaman is, by cultural belief, assigned supernatural power to see the cause of the illness, to know the whereabouts of the vital forces, and to use nuchu spirits who are endowed with exceptional powers to move invisibly and clairvoyantly in the service of humans.

On the surface the song appears rather commonplace among shamanistic cures. The sick woman suffers because she has lost her spiritual double, which constitutes her vital strength. In traveling to the supernatural world and in being aided by assistants in snatching the woman's double from a malevolent spirit and restoring it to its owner, the shaman effects the cure. The exceptional aspect of this song, making it of interest to anthropologists and psychologists alike, is that 'Muu's way' and the abode of Muu are not, to the native mind, simply a mythical itinerary and dwelling-place. They represent, literally, the vagina and uterus of the pregnant woman, which are to be explored by the shaman and nuchu and in whose depths they will wage their victorious combat" (p. 188). In his quest to capture her soul, the shaman also captures other spirits, which govern the vitality of her other body parts (heart, bones, teeth, hair, nails, and feet). Not unlike the invasive attention of the psychotherapist, no body part is left unattended to.

Muu, as instigator of the disorder, has captured the special "souls" of the various organs, thus destroying the cooperation and integrity of the main soul, the woman's double who must be set free. "In a difficult delivery the 'soul' of the uterus has led astray all the 'souls' belonging to other parts of the body. Once these souls are liberated, the soul of the uterus can and must resume its cooperation" (p. 190). It is clear that the song seeks to delineate the emotional content of the physiological disturbance to the mind of the sick woman. To reach Muu, the shaman and his assistants must find 'Muu's way,' the road of Muu. At the peak moment when the shaman has finished his carvings, spirits rise up at the shaman's exhortation:

> The (sick) woman lies in the hammock in front of you.
> Her white tissue lies in her lap, her white tissues move softly. The (sick) woman's body lies weak.
> When they light up (along) Muu's way, it runs over with exudations and like blood.
> Her exudations drip down below the hammock all like blood, all red.
> The inner white tissue extends to the bosom of the earth.
> Into the middle of the woman's white tissue a human being descends. [p. 190]

"Muu's way," darkened and covered with blood, is unquestionably the vagina and the dark whirlpool the uterus where Muu dwells. Lévi-Strauss comments that this text claims a special place among shaman cures. One standard type of cure involves an organ that is manipulated or sucked until a thorn, crystal, or feather appears, a representation of the removal of the malevolent force. Another type of cure revolves around a sham battle waged in a hut and then outside against harmful spirits. In these cures it remains for us to understand exactly how the psychological aspect "hooks into" the physiological. But the current song constitutes a purely psychological treatment. For the shaman does not touch the body and administers no remedy. "Nevertheless it involves, directly and explicitly, the pathological condition and its locus. In our view, the song constitutes a psychological manipulation of the sick organ, and it is precisely from this manipulation that a cure is expected" (p. 192).

Lévi-Strauss observes that the situation is contrived to induce pain in a sick woman through developing a psychological awareness of the smallest details of all of her internal tissues. Using mythological images the pain-induced situation becomes the symbolic setting for the experience of conflict. "A transition will thus be made from the most prosaic reality, to myth, from the physical universe to the psychological universe, from the external world to the internal body" (p. 193). The mythological saga being enacted in the body attains sensory and hallucinatory vividness through the many elements of ritual–smell, sound, tactile stimulation, rhythm, and repetition.

What follows in breathless (hypnotic) rhythm and rhyme are more and more rapid oscillations between mythical and physiological themes "as if to abolish in the mind of the sick woman the distinction which separates them, and to make it impossible to differentiate their respective attributes" (p. 193). Spirits and events follow one another as the woman's total focus becomes the birth apparatus and the cosmic battle being waged there by the invasion of the shaman and his spiritual helpers who bring illuminating light into the birth canal. The presence of wild animals increases the pains that are thus personified and described to the woman. Uncle Alligator moves about with bulging eyes, crouching and wriggling his tail. He moves his glistening flippers that drag on everything. The Octopus arrives with sticky tentacles alternately opening and closing, contracting and expanding passageways. The black tiger, the red animal, the two-colored animals are all tied with an iron chain that rasps and clanks against everything. Their tongues are hanging out, saliva dripping, saliva foaming, with flourishing tails and claws tearing at everything.

According to Lévi-Strauss the cure consists in making explicit a situation originally existing on an emotional level and in rendering acceptable to the mind pains that the body otherwise refuses to tolerate. The shaman with the aid of this myth encourages the woman to accept the incoherent and arbitrary pains, reintegrating them into a whole where everything is coordinated and meaningful. He points out that our physicians tell a similar story to us but not in terms of monsters and spirits but rather in terms we believe like germs, microbes, and so forth. "The shaman provides the sick woman with a language, by means of which unexpressed, and otherwise inexpressible, psychic states can be immediately expressed" (p. 198). The transition to the verbal system makes it possible to undergo in an ordered and intelligible form an experience that would otherwise be chaotic and inexpressible. The myth and its hypnotic power enable the woman to release and reorganize the physiological processes that have become disordered in the woman's sickness.

Lévi-Strauss (1949) explicitly contextualizes this shamanistic cure as psychoanalytic in nature. The purpose is to bring to a conscious level conflicts and resistances that have remained unconscious with resulting symptom formation. The conflicts and resistances are resolved not because of knowledge, real or alleged, but because this knowledge makes possible a specific experience, in the course of which conflicts materialize in an order and on a level permitting their free development and leading to their resolution.

This vital experience is called abreaction in psychoanalysis. We know that its precondition is the unprovoked intervention of the analyst, who appears in the conflicts of the client through a double transference mechanism as (1) a flesh-and-blood protagonist and (2) in relation to whom the client can restore and clarify an initial (historical) situation which has remained unexpressed or unformulated.

The shaman plays the same dual role as the psychoanalyst. A prerequisite role–that of listener for the psychoanalyst and of orator for the shaman–establishes a direct relationship with the patient's conscious and an indirect relationship with her unconscious. This is the function of the incantation proper. But the shaman does more than utter the incantation; he is its hero, for it is he who, at the head of a supernatural battalion of spirits, penetrates the endangered organs and frees the captive soul (pp. 198-199).

The shaman, like the psychoanalyst, is thus enabled by the dual relationship to become (1) the transference object induced vividly in the patient's mind, and (2) the real protagonist of the conflict, which is experienced by the patient as on the border between the physical world and the psychical world. In this dual situation in which pain is deliberately induced by the practitioner, the psychoanalytic client eliminates individual myths by facing the reality of the person of the analyst. And the native woman overcomes an organic disorder by identifying with a mythically transmuted shaman.

Lévi-Strauss notes that the shamarita cure is a counterpart to psychoanalytic cure. Both induce an experience through appeal to myth. The psychoanalytic patient constructs a myth with elements drawn from his or her personal past. The shamanist patient receives from the outside a social myth. In either case the treating person fosters the emergence of a storyline that cures by giving language to experience. The effectiveness of symbols guarantees the parallel development in the process of myth and action.

Lévi-Strauss provides a fascinating argument that aligns the shamanism of ages past with the modern activities of psychoanalysis and psychotherapy. His arguments go considerably beyond Freud and into areas being explored in psychoanalysis and psychotherapy today, in which an inductive property of symbols permits formerly homologous structures built out of different materials at different levels of life-organizational processes, unconscious agency, and rational thought to be understood as profoundly related to one another. Lévi-Strauss points out that the individual vocabulary of the cure is significant only to the extent that the unconscious structures it according to its laws and thus transforms it into language. Whether the myth is a personal re-creation or one borrowed from tradition matters little; *the essential structure of language and the unconscious is the locus of the power of the symbol.* Any myth represents a quest for the remembrance of things past and the ways those remembrances are structured in the unconscious. "The modern version of shamanistic technique called psychoanalysis thus derives its specific characteristics from the fact that in industrial civilization there is no longer any room for mythical time, except within man himself" (pp. 203-204). The intersubjective and relational perspectives for cross-cultural understanding delineated in Part I claim a special relevance to shamarita and psychoanalytic cures with the double action of real relating and symbolization of that relating process.[17]

---

[17] An extended example of Native American or First Nation cure is provided by Puebla Indian Leslie Marmon Silko in her delightful and informative novel Ceremony in which Tao who has experienced a psychotic break while serving in Vietnam is taken back to tribal lands and slowly cured by traditional means

Part IV:
Conclusions

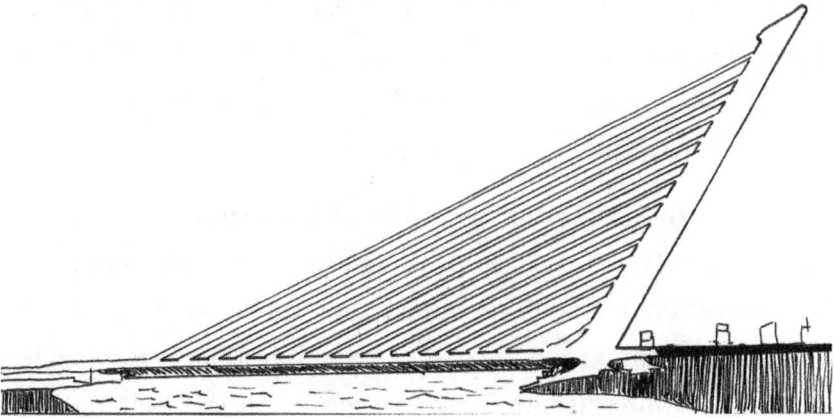

Cross-Culture Encounters: Bridging Worlds of Difference

Today there are clear and unequivocal advantages to being able to operate in multiple cultural codes—as anyone working in a therapeutic, counseling, educational, or business setting knows. There are social, economic, cognitive, and aesthetic advantages to being able to transverse cultural spaces.

Cross-cultural research in attachment, neuroscience, and infant intersubjectivity confirms that Individual, positional, and transgenerational phantoms inhabit our inner worlds, informing us who we are and how we are to be in our relationships and in the world. People raised in different socio-political, economic, and cultural circumstances experience their ghosts differently. Therapeutic, counseling, and educational settings provide opportunities to represent in symbols, language, and enactments the phantoms that inhabit our inner worlds. The task of the professional cannot be to have a knowledge of all of the types of personal, familial, and cultural haunting that diverse people experience. But rather to co-create with the client or student a setting that is maximally conducive to the emergence of internal representations in symbols, words, and actions. For phantoms cannot survive exposure to the light of day!

The "we" and "they" of difference has allowed racism, discrimination, hatred, domination, and privilege of all kinds to exist on social and institutional levels since the beginning of human time. The relationships formed in therapeutic, counseling, and educational settings can promote a process of ongoing dialogue that can work to bridge worlds of difference of the we and they.

While all theories of diagnosis, counseling, education, and therapy are assumed to be culturally biased, cross-cultural professional relational encounters seek to bridge worlds of difference by creating opportunities for dialogue and representation. Common to all healing traditions is the establishment of a relationship followed by a set of interactions aimed at relieving suffering through co-created representations. The universals involved in healing traditions appear to be:

1. The biologically driven attachment need,
2. The socially driven intersubjective exchange, and
3. the neurologically driven affective present moment.

Healers from many traditions have devised ways of tapping into these inherited and learned human characteristics in order to promote beneficial change. In recent years psychotherapy theory and practice has undergone a radical change. The manifold ways in which we now try to grasp the meaning of the unconscious in terms of communication between ourselves and the other subject in the room have opened up the dialogic possibilities of intersubjectivity—nowhere more important than in cross-cultural encounters experienced in various kinds of professional relationships. The evolving dynamics of the mutually co-constructed therapeutic, counseling, and educational relationships allow for the opening of new space and new tensions in which the dance of Thirdness can appear and be jointly negotiated toward mutual regulations and transformations.

Our thoughtful approach to multicultural awareness is a movement toward consciousness-raising about what is going on in the real world around us and where we as a people are going. The point these days is not to eliminate difference, but in our speech and thought to highlight differences as facts without prejudice. Our goal in cross-culture encounters is bridging the gap that exists between people. Bridging involves shooting for the dizzying exhilaration that comes from attaining the mid-position on the bridge, from being able to see each side with some clarity, from knowing that there are two sides and that with help one can manage somehow to negotiate one's way from one side to the other.

Bridging worlds of difference involves achieving a certain sense of mastery that comes from experiencing oneself between separate and different worlds and yet being cognizant of both sides. Building multiple bridges, creating diverse opportunities, inhabiting pluralistic universes—that is our challenge in cross-cultural psychotherapy, counseling, and educational work today.

Multiculturalism is emerging as a "fourth force" in psychology to supplement and ideally strengthen the three historical orientations of humanistic, behavioristic, and psychodynamic psychology "Multiculturalism as a fourth force combines the alternatives of universalism and relativism by explaining behaviors by people from different cultures as simultaneously similar and different.... People are similar in being driven by positive expectations for truth, respect, success, harmony, and positive outcomes that provide the universal values shared across cultures ... [and] People are different to the extent that each culture teaches different behaviors to express those universal expectations.... An inclusive, multicultural, fourth force perspective in therapy, counseling, and educational settings recognizes that similarities and differences coexist.... The Multicultural perspective is not intended to displace or compete with other psychological perspectives, but rather to complement them by framing them in the multicultural contexts in which all psychological interpretation occurs..." (Pedersen 1999, pp. 13-14).

Cultures evolve based on selective mimetics over long periods of time in specific ethnic contexts. Individuals are born into complex mimetic networks which, like complex language networks, are gradually acquired over long periods of time through daily immersion in a web of relationships. Thoughts, feelings, and behavior acquired in mimetic networks are highly resistant to change because human imitation has served to construct living human realities. We have all been "carefully taught" to live within the limits of reality and this includes the limits of our culturally- and ethnically-constructed mimetic realities. This means that a psychotherapist, a counselor, or an educator trying to understand an idea, practice, ritual, or value in the mimetic soup of another is inevitably bound to fail in many regards. As professionals then, simply understanding cultural and ethnic variation cannot possibly be our goal. Rather, we must ask ourselves how we can best position ourselves in our professional settings so that those who live in other mimetic systems can begin to represent, elaborate, and achieve their own understandings of what they are thinking, feeling, or doing themselves in their own life contexts.

The postmodern, social constructionist perspective allows us to consider how cultural constructions create cultural and ethnic realities that become internalized early in life and manifest themselves later in psychotherapeutic, counseling, and educational settings. The postmodern constructionist search to understand human culture involves the study of an infinite array of personal meanings as they become enacted and understood in dynamic relationships, not in finally unearthing the biological, anthropological, or psychological truths about human nature cross-culturally viewed. That is, in exploring the many complex, affective, and interpersonal aspects of anyone's cultural and/or ethnic orientations, therapists, counselors, and educators must be able to do more than simply explore the behavior and personal narratives put before them. Rather, *through the interpersonal engagement of the professional relationship itself*, there emerges the possibility for

1. co-constructing new more encompassing interpersonal narratives,

2. engaging in novel interpersonal encounters, and

3. mutually creating fresh meanings of experiences of culture and ethnicity.

The listening perspective that links ethnicity and sexuality views sex as a core constitutive element of race, ethnicity, and the nation; and that race, ethnicity and nationalism are crucial components of sexual and moral boundaries and systems. In psychotherapy, counseling, and education beyond what is consciously and explicitly presented, the professional has the additional task of being alert to how many different kinds of ethnicity and sexuality are embedded in each person's conscious and unconscious histories, and how in the professional relationship itself new erotics are continuously being mutually co-constructed based on the ethnic and sexuality dimensions both participants bring to a professional relationship.

The evolving dynamics of the mutually co-constructed therapeutic, counseling, or educational relationship allow for the opening of new space and new tensions in which the dance of Thirdness can appear and be jointly negotiated toward mutual regulations and transformations.

We can no longer simply take anyone's stated cultural, ethnic, or sexual orientations or gender identities at face value in life or in psychotherapy. Through cross-cultural encounters we seek to bridge worlds of difference while remaining ever mindful of the personal and cultural biases both participants bring to the relationship.

References

Allen, W. T. (1997). *The Invention of the White Race: The Origin of Racial Oppression in Anglo-America*. Vol. 2. Verso: London • New York

Altman, N. (1995). *The Analyst in the Inner City*. New York: The Analytic Press.

___(1996). The accommodation of diversity in psychoanalysis. In Foster, R. P., Moskowitz, M., and Javier, R. A. (Eds.). *Reaching Across Boundaries of Culture and Class: Widening the Scope of Psychotherapy*. Lanham, MD: Rowman & Littlefield Publishers.

Backenroth-Ohsako, G. A. M. (1999). Multiculturalism and the deaf community: Examples given from deaf people working in bicultural groups. In Pederson, P. (1999). *Multiculturalism as a Fourth Force*. Philadelphia: Brunner Mazel.

Beck, E. T., Goldberg, J. L., and Knefelkamp, L. L. (2003). Integrating Jewish issues into the teaching of psychology. In P. Bronstein and K. Quina (Eds.). *Teaching Gender and Multicultural Awareness: Resources for the Psychology Classroom* (pp. 237-252). Washington, D.C.: American Psychological Association.

Cushman, P. (1995). *Constructing the Self, Constructing America: A Cultural History of Psychotherapy*. Cambridge, MA: Perseus Publishing.

Doi, T. (1988). *The Anatomy of Self: The Individual Versus Society* (M. A. Harbison, Trans.). Tokyo: Kodansha International. (Original work published 1985).

Foster, R. P., Moskowitz, M., and Javier, R. A. (Eds.). (1996). *Reaching Across Boundaries of Culture and Class: Widening the Scope of Psychotherapy*. Lanham, MD: Rowman & Littlefield Publishers.

Franklin, N. B. (2003). *Black Families in Therapy: Understanding the African American Experience* (2nd Edition). New York: The Guilford Press.

Franklin, J. A. (2002). *From Brotherhood to Manhood: How Black Men Rescue Their Relationships and Dreams from the Invisibility Syndrome.* New York: Wiley.

Gill, E. (2005). "From Sensitivity to Competence in Working across Cultures" In E. Gill & A. A. Drewes. *Cultural Issues in Play Therapy.* New York. The Guildford Press

Hedges, L. E. (1983; 2003). *Listening Perspectives in Psychotherapy.* New Jersey: Aronson.

____(1994). *Remembering, Repeating and Working Through Childhood Trauma: The Psychodynamics of Recovered Memories, Multiple Personality, Ritual Abuse, Incest, Molest and Abduction.* New Jersey: Aronson, pp. 161-170.

____(2000). Terrifying Transferences: Aftershocks of Childhood Trauma. New Jersey: Aronson.

hooks, bell. (1995). *Killing Rage: Ending Racism.* Henry Holt and Company: New York.

Karr-Morse, R., and Wiley, M. S. (1997). *Ghosts from the Nursery: Tracing the Roots of Violence.* New York: The Atlantic Monthly Press.

Lee, E. (Ed.). (1997). *Working with Asian Americans: A Guide for Clinicians.* New York: The Guilford Press.

Levine, P., and Frederick, A. (1997). *Waking the Tiger: Healing Trauma: The Innate Capacity to Transform Overwhelming Experiences.* North Atlantic Books.

Loo, C. M. (1998). *Chinese America: Mental Health and Quality of Life in the Inner City.* Sage Publications: Thousand Oaks, London and New Delhi.

Mishne, J. (2002). *Multiculturalism and the Therapeutic Process.* New York/London: The Guilford Press.

Moss, D. (Ed.). (2003). *Hating in the First Person Plural*. New York: Other Press.

Nagel, J. (1996). *American Indian Ethnic Renewal: Red Power and the Resurgence of Identity and Culture*. Oxford University Press.

____(2003). *Race, Ethnicity, and Sexuality: Intimate Intersections, Forbidden Frontiers*. Oxford University Press

Pack-Brown, S. P., and Williams, C. B. (2003). *Ethics in a Multicultural Context*. Thousand Oaks, CA: Sage Publications.

Pederson, P. (1999). *Multiculturalism as a Fourth Force*. Department of Human Studies, School of Education: University of Alabama Birmingham.

Richardson, B. L. and Wade, B. (2000). *What Mama Couldn't Tell Us About Love: Healing the Emotional Legacy of Slavery by Celebrating Our Light*. Perennial: Harper Collins Publishers.

Ridley, C. (1995). *Overcoming Unintentional Racism in Counseling and Therapy: A Practitioner's Guide to Intentional Intervention*. Sage Publications: International Educational and Professional Publisher.

Rodriguez, L. J. (1993). *Always Running: La Vida Loca: Gang Days in L.A.* New York: Touchstone Books.

Roland, A. (1988). *In Search of Self in India and Japan: Toward a Cross-Cultural Psychology*. Princeton University Press.

____(1996). How universal is the psychoanalytic self? In Foster, R. P., Moskowitz, M., and Javier, R. A. (Eds.). *Reaching Across Boundaries of Culture and Class: Widening the Scope of Psychotherapy*. Lanham, MD: Rowman & Littlefield Publishers.

Silko, L. M. (1977). *Ceremony*. New York: Penguin.

Suárez-Orozco, C., & Suárez-Orozco, M. M. (2001). *Children of Immigration. Cambridge*. MA: Harvard University Press.

Sue, D. W. (2003). *Overcoming Our Racism: The Journey to Liberation*. San Francisco: Jossey-Bass.

____(Ed.). (1998). *Multicultural Counseling Competencies: Individual and Organizational Development* (Multicultural

Aspects of Counseling Series, Vol. 11). Thousand Oaks, CA: Sage Publications.

Sue, D. W., Ivey, A. E., and Pedersen, P. B. (Eds.). (1996). *A Theory of Multicultural Counseling and Therapy*. Pacific Grove, CA: Brooks/Cole Publishing Company.

Thompson, C. L. (1996). The African-American patient in psychodynamic treatment. In Foster, R. P., Moskowitz, M., and Javier, R. A. (Eds.). *Reaching Across Boundaries of Culture and Class: Widening the Scope of Psychotherapy*. Lanham, MD: Rowman & Littlefield Publishers.

Volkan, V. (2004). *Blind Trust: Large Groups and Their Leaders in Time of Crisis and Terror*. Charlottesville, VA: Pitchstone Publishing.

West, C. (1993/2001). *Race Matters*. New York: Vintage Books.

Young-Bruehl, E. (1998). *The Anatomy of Prejudices*. Cambridge: Harvard University Press.

About the Author

Lawrence Hedges, Ph.D., Psy.D., ABPP, began seeing patients in 1966 and completed his training in child psychoanalysis in 1973. Since that time his primary occupation has been training and supervising psychotherapists, individually and in groups, on their most difficult cases at the Listening Perspectives Study Center in Orange, California. Dr. Hedges was the Founding Director of the Newport Psychoanalytic Institute in 1983, where he continues to serve as a supervising and training analyst. Throughout his career, Dr. Hedges has provided continuing education courses for psychotherapists throughout the United States and abroad. He has consulted or served as expert witness on more than 400 complaints against psychotherapists in 20 states and has published 23 books on various topics of interest to psychoanalysts and psychoanalytic psychotherapists, three of which have received the Gradiva Award for the best psychoanalytic book of the year. During the 2009 centennial celebration of the International Psychoanalytic Association, his 1992 book, *Interpreting the Countertransference*, was named one of the key contributions in the relational track during the first century of psychoanalytics. In 2015 Dr. Hedges was distinguished by being awarded honorary membership in the American Psychoanalytic Association for his many contributions to psychoanalysis through the years.

Photograph courtesy Marcie Bell

Other Books Authored and Edited by Lawrence Hedges

Listening Perspectives in Psychotherapy (1983; Revised Edition 2003; 40th Anniversary Edition 2022)

In a fresh and innovative format Hedges organizes an exhaustive overview of contemporary psychoanalytic and object relations theory and clinical practice. "In studying the Listening Perspectives of therapists, the author has identified himself with the idea that one must sometimes change the Listening Perspective and also the interpreting, responding perspective." –Rudolf Ekstein, Ph.D. Contributing therapists: Mary Cook, Susan Courtney, Charles Coverdale, Arlene Dorius, David Garland, Charles Margach, Jenna Riley, and Mary E. Walker. Now available in a 40th Anniversary edition, the book has become a classic in the field.

Interpreting the Countertransference (1992)

Hedges boldly studies countertransference as a critical tool for therapeutic understanding. As Dr. James Grotstein notes, "Hedges clearly and beautifully delineates the components and forms of countertransference and explicates the technique of carefully proffered countertransference informed interventions ... [He takes the view] that all countertransferences, no matter how much they belong to the analyst, are unconsciously evoked by the patient." Contributing therapists: Anthony Brailow, Karen K. Redding, and Howard Rogers. During the 2009 centennial celebrations of The International Psychoanalytic Association his 1992 book, Interpreting the Countertransference, was named one of the key contributions in the relational track during the first century of psychoanalytics.

In Search of the Lost Mother of Infancy (1994)

"Organizing transferences" in psychotherapy constitute a living memory of a person's earliest relatedness experiences and failures. Infant research and psychotherapeutic studies from the past two decades now make it possible to define for therapeutic analysis the manifestations of early contact traumas. A history and summary of the Listening Perspective approach to psychotherapy introduces the book. Contributing therapists: Bill Cone, Cecile Dillon, Francie Marais, Sandra Russell, Sabrina Salayz, Jacki Singer, Sean Stewart, Ruth Wimsatt, and Marina Young.

Remembering, Repeating, and Working Through Childhood Trauma:
The Psychodynamics of Recovered Memories, Multiple Personality,
Ritual Abuse, Incest, Molest, and Abduction (1994)

Infantile focal as well as strain trauma leave deep psychological scars that show up as symptoms and memories later in life. In psychotherapy people seek to process early experiences that lack ordinary pictoral and narrational representations through a variety of forms of transference and dissociative remembering such as multiple personality, dual relating, archetypal adventures, and false accusations against therapists or other emotionally significant people. "Lawrence Hedges makes a powerful and compelling argument for why traumatic memories recovered during psychotherapy need to be taken seriously," says Elizabeth F. Loftus, Ph.D. "He shows us how and why these memories must be dealt with in thoughtful and responsible ways and not simply uncritically believed and used as tools for destruction." Nominated for Gradiva Best Book of the Year Award.

Working the Organizing Experience:
Transforming Psychotic, Schizoid, and Autistic States (1994)

Hedges defines in a clear and impelling manner the most fundamental and treacherous transference phenomena, the emotional experiences retained from the first few months of life. Hedges describes the infant's attempts to reach out and form organizing connections to the interpersonal environment and how those attempts may have been ignored, thwarted, and/or rejected. He demonstrates how people live out these primitive transferences in everyday significant relationships and in the psychotherapy relationship. A critical history of psychotherapy with primitive transferences is contributed by James Grotstein and a case study is contributed by Frances Tustin.

Strategic Emotional Involvement:
Using the Countertransference in Psychotherapy (1996)

Following an overview of contemporary approaches to studying countertransference responsiveness, therapists tell moving stories of how their work came to involve them deeply, emotionally, and not always safely with clients. These comprehensive, intense, and honest reports are the first of their kind ever to be collected and published. Contributing therapists: Anthony Brailow, Suzanne Buchanan, Charles Coverdale, Carolyn Crawford, Jolyn Davidson, Jacqueline Gillespie, Ronald Hirz, Virginia Hunter, Gayle Trenberth, and Sally Turner-Miller.

Therapists at Risk: Perils of the Intimacy of the Therapeutic Relationship (1997)

Lawrence E. Hedges, Robert Hilton, and Virginia Wink Hilton, long-time trainers of psychotherapists, join hands with attorney O. Brandt Caudill in this *tour de force* which explores the multitude of personal, ethical, and legal risks involved in achieving rewarding transformative connections in psychotherapy today. Relational intimacy is explored through such issues as touching, dualities in relationship, interfacing boundaries, sexuality, countertransference, recovered memories, primitive transferences, false accusations against therapists, and the critical importance of peer support and consultation. The authors clarify the many dynamic issues involved, suggest useful ways of managing the inherent dangers, and work to restore our confidence in and natural enjoyment of the psychotherapeutic process.

Facing the Challenge of Liability in Psychotherapy: Practicing Defensively (2000; Revised 2017)

In this litigious age, all psychotherapists must protect themselves against the possibility of legal action; malpractice insurance is insufficient and does not begin to address the complexity and the enormity of this critical problem. In this book, Lawrence E. Hedges urges clinicians to practice defensively and provides a course of action that equips them to do so. After working with over a hundred psycho-therapists and attorneys who have fought unwarranted legal and ethical complaints from clients, he has made the fruits of his work available to all therapists. In addition to identifying those patients prone to presenting legal problems, Dr. Hedges provides a series of consent forms (on the accompanying disk), a compelling rationale for using them, and a means of easily introducing them into clinical practice. This book is a wake-up call, a practical, clinically sound response to a frightening reality, and an absolute necessity for all therapists in practice today. Now available in a revised and updated edition. Gradiva Award Best Book of the Year.

Terrifying Transferences: Aftershocks of Childhood Trauma (2000)

There is a level of stark terror known to one degree or another by all human beings. It silently haunts our lives and occasionally surfaces in therapy. It is this deep-seated fear—often manifest in dreams or fantasies of dismemberment, mutilation, torture, abuse, insanity, rape, or death—that grips us with the terror of being lost forever in time and space or controlled by hostile forces stronger than ourselves. Whether the terror is felt by the client or by the therapist, it has a disorienting, fragmenting, crippling power. How we can look directly into the face of such terror, hold steady, and safely work it through is the subject of *Terrifying Transferences*. Contributing therapists: Linda Barnhurst, John Carter, Shirley Cox, Jolyn Davidson, Virginia Hunter, Michael Reyes, Audrey Seaton-Bacon, Sean Stewart, Gayle Trenberth, and Cynthia Wygal. Gradiva Award Best Book of the Year.

Sex in Psychotherapy: Sexuality, Passion, Love, and Desire in the Therapeutic Encounter (2010)

This book takes a psychodynamic approach to understanding recent technological and theoretical shifts in the field of psychotherapy. Hedges provides an expert overview and analysis of a wide variety of new perspectives on sex, sexuality, gender, and identity; new theories about sex's role in therapy; and new discoveries about the human brain and how it works. Therapists will value Hedges's unique insights into the role of sexuality in therapy, which are grounded in the author's studies of neurology, the history of sexuality, transference, resistance, and countertransference. Clinicians will also appreciate his provocative analyses of influential perspectives on sex, gender, and identity, and his lucid, concrete advice on the practice of therapeutic listening. This is an explosive work of tremendous imagination and scholarship. Hedges speaks the uncomfortable truth that psychotherapy today often reinforces the very paradigms that keep patients stuck in self-defeating, frustrating behavior. He sees sexuality as a vehicle for both therapists and patients to challenge what they think they know about the nature of self and intimacy. This book is a must-read for anyone interested in understanding 21st-century human beings—or in better understanding themselves and their sexuality.

Overcoming Our Relationship Fears (2012)

We are all aware that chronic tension saps our energy and contributes to such modern maladies as high blood pressure and tension headaches, but few of us realize that this is caused by muscle constrictions that started as relationship fears in early childhood and live on in our minds and bodies. Overcoming Our Relationship Fears is a user-friendly roadmap for healing our relationships by dealing with our childhood fear reflexes. It is replete with relationship stories to illustrate each fear and how we individually express them. Dr. Hedges shows how to use our own built-in "Aliveness Monitor" to gauge our body's reaction to daily interactions and how they trigger our fears. Exercises in the book will help us release these life-threatening constrictions and reclaim our aliveness with ourselves and others.

Overcoming Our Relationship Fears: WORKBOOK (2013)

Developed to accompany Hedges's Overcoming Relationship Fears, this workbook contains a general introduction to the seven relationship fears that are a part of normal human development along with a series of exercises for individuals and couples who wish to learn to how to release their Body-Mind-Relationship fear reflexes. An Aliveness Journal is provided for charting the way these fears manifest in relationships and body maps to chart their location in each person's body.

The Relationship in Psychotherapy and Supervision (2013)

The sea-change in our understanding of neurobiology, infant research, and interpersonal/relational psychology over the past two decades makes clear that we are first and foremost a relational species. This finding has massive implications for the relational processes involved in teaching and supervising psychotherapy. Clinical theory and technique can be taught didactically. But relationship can only be learned through careful attention to the supervisory encounter itself. This advanced text surveys the psychodynamic and relational processes involved in psychotherapy and supervision.

Making Love Last: Creating and Maintaining Intimacy in Long-term Relationships (2013)

We have long known that physical and emotional intimacy diminish during the course of long-term relationships. This book deals with the questions, "Why romance fades over time?" And "What can we do about it?" Relational psychologists, neuropsychologists, and anthropologists have devoted the last two decades to the study of these questions with never before available research tools. It is now clear that we are genetically predisposed to search out intersubjective intimacy from birth but that cultural systems of child rearing seriously limit our possibilities for rewarding interpersonal relationships. Anthropological and neurological data suggests that over time we have been essentially a serially monogamous species with an extraordinary capacity for carving out new destinies for ourselves. How can we come to grips with our genetic and neurological heritage while simultaneously transcending our relational history in order to create and sustain exciting romance and nurturing love in long-term relationships? Making Love Last surveys research and theory suggesting that indeed we have the capacity and the means of achieving the lasting love we long for in our committed relationships.

Relational Interventions:
Treating Borderline, Bipolar, Schizophrenic, Psychotic, and Characterological Personality Organization (2013)

Many clinicians dread working with individuals diagnosed as borderline, bipolar, schizophrenic, psychotic, and character disordered. Often labeled as "high risk" or "difficult", these relational problems and their interpersonal manifestations often require long and intense transformative therapy. In this book Dr. Hedges explains how to address the nature of personality organization in order to flow with—and eventually to enjoy—working at early developmental levels. Dr. Hedges speaks to the client's engagement/disengagement needs, using a relational process-oriented approach, so the therapist can gauge how much and what kind of therapy can be achieved at any point and time.

Facing Our Cumulative Developmental Traumas (2015)

It has now become clear that Cumulative Developmental Trauma is universal. That is, there is no way to grow up and walk the planet without being repeatedly swallowed up by emotional and relational demands from other people. When we become confused, frightened, and overwhelmed our conscious and unconscious minds seek remedies to deal with the situation. Unfortunately, many of the solutions developed in response to intrusive events turn into habitual fear reflexes that get in our way later in life, giving rise to post traumatic stress and relational inhibitions…. This book is about freeing ourselves from the cumulative effects of our life's many relational traumas and the after-effects of those traumas that continue to constrict our capacities for creative, spontaneous, and passionate living.

Relational Listening: A Handbook

Freud's singular stroke of genius can be simply stated: *When we engage with someone in an emotionally intimate relationship, the deep unconscious emotional/relational habits of both participants become interpersonally engaged and enacted thereby making them potentially available for notice, discussion, transformation, and expansion.*

This *Handbook* is the 20th book in a series edited and/or authored by Dr. Lawrence Hedges and surveys a massive clinical research project extending over 45 years and participated in by more than 400 psychotherapists in case conferences, reading groups and seminars at the Listening Perspectives Study Center and the Newport Psychoanalytic Institute in the Southern California area. The first book in the series, *Listening Perspectives in Psychotherapy* (1983), was widely praised for its comprehensive survey of 100 years of psychoanalytic studies and a

20th anniversary edition was published in 2003. But the important aspect of the book—that the studies were organized according to four different forms of relational listening according to different levels of developmental complexity—went largely unnoticed. Also generally unattended was the critical epistemological shift to perspectivalism which since that time has become better understood. The subsequent books participated in by numerous therapists expand and elaborate these *Relational Listening* perspectives for working clinicians. This *Handbook* provides not only a survey of the findings of the 45-year clinical research project but, more importantly, an overview of the seven developmental levels of relational listening that have consistently been found to provide enhanced psychotherapeutic engagement.

The Call of Darkness:
A Relational Listening Approach to Suicide Intervention (2018)

The White House has declared suicide to be a national and international epidemic and has mandated suicide prevention training for educational and health workers nationwide. *The Call of Darkness* was written in response to that mandate and begins with the awareness that our ability to predict suicide is little better than chance and that at present there are no consistently reliable empirically validated treatment techniques to prevent suicide. However, in the past three decades much has been learned about the dynamics of suicide and promising treatment approaches have been advanced that are slowly yielding clinical as well as empirical results.

In this book, Dr. Hedges presents the groundbreaking work on suicidality of Freud, Jung, Menninger and Shneidman as well as the more recent work of Linehan, Kernberg, Joiner and the attachment theorists along with the features in common that these treatment approaches seem to share. He puts forth a Relational Listening approach regarding the origins of suicidality in a relational/ developmental context and will consider their implications for treating, and managing suicidality. The tendencies towards blame and self-blame on the part of survivors raise issues of professional responsibility. Dr Hedges discusses accurate assessment, thorough documentation, appropriate standards of care, and liability management.

Terror in Psychotherapy: The New Zealand Lectures (2020)

Contemporary neuroscience, infant research, and relational psychotherapy make clear that we are a relational species—that our brain and neurological systems actually organize in the first year of life depending on the relationships that are and are not available. By the second year of life a symbiotic interaction, characterized by mutual affect regulation and mutual attachment experiences, is becoming established. In Terror in Psychotherapy, Dr. Lawrence Hedges demonstrates how trauma experienced during these "organizing" and "symbiotic" levels of relational development stimulate fear, anxiety, and terror that have consequences for later relationships—in extreme forms laying the foundation for suicide and homicide. A series of case vignettes illustrate how early relational intrusive trauma produce terror in transference and countertransference experiencing.

The Relational Approach in Psychotherapy: The China Lectures (2023)

Although virtually all psychological theories and schools of thought now acknowledge the importance of the relationship in psychotherapy, the relationship itself is conceptualized in various ways. In this book, a ten-lecture series presented in ZhengDou, China as a continuing education program to hundreds of psychotherapists, Dr. Larry Hedges surveys a 50-year clinical research program into the nature of relationship based on the therapeutic experience of and contributions from over 400 practitioners.

www.ingramcontent.com/pod-product-compliance
Lightning Source LLC
Chambersburg PA
CBHW031513270326

41930CB00006B/384